Understanding

MIND · BODY · AND SPIRIT

Stress

Understanding

MIND · BODY · AND SPIRIT

Stress

**GEDDES &
GROSSET**

Published by Geddes & Grosset, an imprint of
Children's Leisure Products Limited

© 1996 Children's Leisure Products Limited,
David Dale House, New Lanark, ML11 9DJ, Scotland

First published 1996
Reprinted 1999

ISBN 1 85534 239 1

Printed and bound in the UK

Contents

PART ONE

The Nature of Stress

What is stress?

Stress is the 'wear and tear' our minds and bodies experience as we attempt to cope with our continually changing environment. People often think of stress as pressure at work, a sick child or rush-hour traffic. These events may be triggers, but stress is actually the body's internal reaction to such factors. Stress is the automatic 'fight-or-flight' response in the body, activated by adrenaline and other stress hormones, which stimulate a variety of physiological changes, such as increased heart rate and blood pressure, faster breathing, muscle tension, dilated pupils, dry mouth and increased blood sugar. In simple biological terms, stress is the state of increased arousal necessary for an organism to defend itself when faced with danger.

Whenever we feel anxious, tense, tired, frightened, elated or depressed, we are undergoing stress. Few aspects of life are free from the events and pressures that generate such feelings, and stress has become an acceptable and unavoidable part of normal everyday existence. In fact, contrary to popular assumptions, stressed lifestyles are not an exclusively modern phenomenon – stress has *always* been intrinsic to human existence, and life without stress would be unbearable. For example, certain types of stress, such as physical and mental exercise, sex, and intense creativity, are actually very desirable. It is only when real or perceived change overwhelms the body's ability to cope, that stress becomes harmful (distress), leaving us prone to unwanted physical, mental or emotional reactions and illnesses.

Types of stress

The causes of stress ('stressors') are multiple and varied, but they can be divided into two general categories – external and internal:

External stressors

- *physical environment* – noise, bright lights, heat, confined spaces

- *social interaction* – rudeness, bossiness or aggressiveness by others

- *organisational* – rules, regulations, 'red tape', deadlines

- *major life events* – death of a relative, lost job, promotion, new baby

- *daily hassles* – commuting, misplacing keys, mechanical breakdowns

Internal stressors

- *lifestyle choices* – caffeine, not enough sleep, overloaded schedule

- *negative self-talk* – pessimistic thinking, self-criticism, over-analysing

- *mind traps* – unrealistic expectations, taking things personally, all-or-nothing thinking, exaggerating, rigid thinking

- *stressful personality traits* – type A, perfectionist, workaholic

These factors generate various symptoms of emotional and mental stress, the most common including:

- anger
- anxiety
- worry
- fear
- depression

Negative stress

Excessive, prolonged and unrelieved stress can have a harmful effect on mental, physical and spiritual health. If left unresolved, the feelings of anger, frustration, fear and depression generated by stress can trigger a variety of illnesses. It is estimated that stress is the most common cause of ill health in modern society, probably underlying as many as 80 per cent of all visits to family doctors. Stress is a contributory factor in relatively minor conditions, such as headaches, digestive problems, skin complaints, insomnia and ulcers, but also plays an important role in the leading causes of death in the western world – cancer, cardiovascular disease, respiratory disorders, accidental injuries, cirrhosis of the liver and suicide.

Positive stress

Stress can also have a positive effect. It is essential in spurring motivation and awareness, providing the stimulation needed to cope with challenging situations. Tension and arousal are necessary for the enjoyment of many aspects of life, and without them existence would be pretty dull. Stress also provides the sense of urgency and alertness needed for survival when confronting threatening situations, such as crossing a busy road or driving in poor weather conditions.

An overly relaxed approach in such situations could be fatal.

Stress and the individual

There is no single level of stress that is optimal for all people. Everyone is different, with unique perceptions of, and reactions to, events: what is distressing to one person may be a joy to another. A person who loves to work alone would be stressed in a job that involved high levels of social interaction, whereas the person who thrives as part of a team would very likely be stressed in a job that involved working from home.

Even when we agree that a particular event is distressing, we are likely to differ in our physiological and psychological responses to it. Some individuals are more sensitive to stress than others, owing to experiences in childhood and the influence of teachers, parents, religion, etc. It is also important to note that most of the stress that we experience is actually *self-generated*. How we perceive life – whether an event makes

The Cost of Stress

- It is estimated that 80 per cent of all modern diseases have their origins in stress.
- In the UK 40 million working days are lost per year directly from stress-related illnesses.
- The cost in absenteeism to British industry from stress-related illnesses, such as migraine, alcohol abuse, etc, is estimated at £1.5 billion per year.
- In the UK 250,000 people die annually from coronary heart disease.
- The estimated medical costs of stress in the USA are well over $1 billion per year.
- In the USA, heart disease has increased 500 per cent over the last 50 years.
- Americans take 5 billion doses of tranquillizers and 16,000 tons of aspirin each year.

us feel threatened or stimulated, encouraged or discouraged, happy or sad – depends to a large extent on how we perceive ourselves.

Self-generated stress is something of a paradox, because so many people think of external causes when they are upset. Recognising that we create most of our own upsets is an important first step towards coping with them.

The stress response

How our bodies respond to stress was first described in the 1930s by two American doctors, Walter B. Cannon and Hans Selye. They found that the first reaction to severe stress is what is known as the 'fight-or-flight' response, which activates the body's protective mechanism either to fight (confront the stressor) or flee (act to avoid the stressor or threat of it). Initially, the fight-or-flight response alerts us to danger and is, in fact, beneficial – providing the strength, speed and stamina necessary for survival.

The stress response is controlled by the endocrine system, which regulates various bodily functions, including the reproductive system, the immune system, growth, metabolism, allergic response and stress tolerance. Any unusual demand on the body's physical and mental resources stimulates the endocrine glands – mainly the adrenal, pituitary and hypothalamus – to secrete chemical messengers, called hormones, into the blood stream. These stress hormones include powerful stimulants, such as adrenaline, noradrenaline, cortisol, testosterone and thyroxin, which produce a variety of physical responses. The most common include:

- increased pupil dilation

- perspiration

- increased heart rate and blood pressure (to get more blood to the muscles, brain and heart)

- rapid breathing (to take in more oxygen)

- muscle tenseness (in preparation for action)

- increased blood flow to the brain, heart and

muscles (the organs that are most important in dealing with danger)

- less blood flow to the skin, digestive tract, kidneys and liver (where it is least needed in times of crisis)

- increased mental alertness and sensitivity (to assess the situation and act quickly)

- increased blood sugar, fats and cholesterol (for extra energy)

- a rise in platelets and blood-clotting factors (to prevent haemorrhage in case of injury)

Unfortunately, although this natural physical response would have been invaluable at an earlier stage in human evolution, fighting and running away are rarely appropriate responses to stressful situations in the modern world. Under long term, unrelieved stress our bodies remain in a constant state of arousal, which can result in the gradual onset of various health problems.

General Adaptation Syndrome

How the body adapts to prolonged stress is described by Dr Hans Selye in terms of the General Adaptation Syndrome. Selye divides the stress response into three phases: the Alarm Response, Adaptation, and Exhaustion. The Alarm Response is the fight-or-flight response that prepares the body for immediate action. If the source of stress persists, then the body prepares for long-term protection through the secretion of further hormones that increase blood sugar levels to sustain energy and raise blood pressure. This Adaptation phase, resulting from exposure to prolonged periods of stress, is common, and not necessarily harmful, but without periods of relaxation and rest to counterbalance the stress response, sufferers become prone to fatigue, concentration lapses, irritability and lethargy as the effort to sustain arousal slides into negative stress. Under persistent chronic stress, sufferers enter the Exhaustion phase: mental, physical and emotional resources suffer heavily, and the body experiences 'adrenal exhaustion', where blood sugar levels decrease as the adrenals become depleted, leading to decreased stress tolerance, progressive mental and physical exhaustion, illness and collapse.

Symptoms of stress

Constant exposure to excessive stress results in hormonal imbalances, which can produce a variety of symptoms:

Physical symptoms

- changes in sleep patterns
- fatigue
- changes in digestion – nausea, vomiting, diarrhoea
- loss of sexual drive
- headaches
- aches and pains in different areas of the body
- infections

The Stress Response

Physical Reaction

Brain sends biochemical message that triggers adrenal gland

Pupils dilate

Mouth goes dry

Neck and shoulder muscles tense – large skeletal muscles contract, ready for action

Breathing becomes faster and shallower, supplying more oxygen to muscles

Heart pumps faster and blood pressure rises

Liver releases stored sugar to provide fuel for quick energy

Adrenaline and noradrenaline released

Digestion slows down or stops as blood is diverted away from the stomach

The body cools itself by perspiring: blood vessels and capillaries move close to skin surface

Muscles at opening of anus and bladder are relaxed

Symptom

Headaches, dizziness

Blurred vision

Difficulty swallowing

Aching neck, backache

Over-breathing, chest pains, tingling, palpitations, asthma

High blood pressure

Excess sugar in blood, indigestion

Nausea, indigestion, ulcers

Excess sweating, blushing

Frequent urination, diarrhoea

- indigestion
- dizziness, faintness, sweating and trembling
- tingling of hands and feet
- breathlessness
- palpitations
- missed heartbeats

Mental symptoms
- lack of concentration
- memory lapses
- difficulty in making decisions
- confusion
- disorientation
- panic attacks

Behavioural symptoms
- appetite changes – eating too much or too little
- eating disorders – anorexia, bulimia

- increased intake of alcohol and other drugs
- increased smoking
- restlessness
- fidgeting
- nail-biting
- hypochondria

Emotional symptoms
- bouts of depression
- impatience and irritability
- fits of rage
- tearfulness
- deterioration in personal hygiene and appearance

Stress-related illness
Cardiovascular disease
The term 'cardiovascular' refers to the heart and to the body's system of blood vessels.

Cardiovascular disease is probably the most serious health problem that can be linked to stress – it is the most common cause of death in Britain and the USA. The primary causes of heart disease include smoking and high-fat diets, but stress is a significant contributory factor.

Adrenal hormones act to increase blood pressure; temporary rises in blood pressure present no threat to health, but a frequent or perpetual state of high blood pressure can have a serious effect on health in the long term. High blood pressure is linked with the development of arteriosclerosis, or hardening of the arteries. Arteriosclerosis is the result of the development of blood plaque in the arteries, which progressively narrows the pathway through which the blood flows. Eventually an artery can become blocked, leading to angina, stroke and heart failure.

The immune system
The immune system protects the body from infection. It fights foreign invaders (such as vi-

ruses and harmful bacteria) and cancer. Excessive stress can damage the immune system by affecting the thymus gland. This manufactures white blood cells, called T-cells, for regulating immunity and also produces various immune-related hormones. The stress reaction diverts resources to the main parts of the body that need to deal with stress, mainly the brain, heart and muscles. Other systems are deprived of resources, including the immune system. Hormones produced by the adrenal glands can cause the thymus gland to shrink and also degrade the activity of white blood cells, causing damage to the body's ability to fight infection. As a result high stress can result in reduced resistance to common infections, such as colds, influenza and herpes (cold sores). Because certain types of white blood cells produced by the thymus are active in preventing the development of cancer cells in the body, any damage to the thymus may effect the body's ability to resist cancer.

Asthma

Asthma is a respiratory disorder marked by the temporary constriction of the bronchi, the airways branching from the trachea to the lungs. Attacks usually are brought on by allergic reaction to antigens, such as grass and tree pollens, mould spores, fungi, animal dander, and certain foods, but may also be caused by chemical irritants in the atmosphere or by infections of the respiratory tract. Susceptibility to an asthma attack is based on hyperactivity of the bronchial muscles, which constrict on exposure to one or other of these agents. Chronic stress reduces the efficiency of the adrenal glands, reducing the output of anti-inflammatory and anti-allergic adrenal hormones, which may make an asthma attack more likely.

Diabetes

Diabetes is caused by the inability of the body to metabolise sugar correctly, leading to excessively high levels of sugar in the blood. Sugar metabolism is the responsibility of the hormone insulin, which is secreted by the pancreas. Most diabetics can produce insulin, but various factors limit the hormone's efficiency, known as 'insulin sensitivity'.

As we know from the physiology of the stress response, the release of adrenal hormones under stress can have significant impact on blood-sugar levels. Adrenaline causes sugar in the liver to be dumped into the blood stream, and cortisol acts to reduce metabolism of glucose by cells. Large amounts of cortisol act to decrease insulin sensitivity. High blood-sugar levels are not dangerous in normally healthy individuals, but chronic stress, combined with other factors such as obesity, act to increase the likelihood of developing diabetes.

Ulcers

Ulcers are frequently associated with stress, although no conclusive link has yet been demonstrated. Normally the lining of the stomach is covered with a layer of mucus to protect it from the digestive acids and enzymes used in the breaking down of food. Over time, chronic stress can stimulate the overproduction of gastric juices, which break down the protective mucus and act upon the walls of the digestive tract, resulting in ulceration. Ulcers usually occur singly as round or oval lesions; the erosions are usually shallow but can penetrate the entire wall, leading to haemorrhage and possibly death.

Digestive disorders

Many problems with the digestive tract, such as constipation, diarrhoea and irritable bowel syndrome, are linked to stress. The nerves in the digestive tract receive messages from the brain in the form of hormones, which tell the intestinal muscles to expand or contract. Hormonal imbalances can cause alterations in intestinal function, such as spasms, constipation and diarrhoea. Chronic stress tends to shut down the digestive system altogether, exacerbating intestinal problems.

Skin complaints
Stress increases levels of toxicity in the body and contributes to hormonal imbalances, both of which have an effect on the skin. The visible effects of stress on the skin include:

- acne
- spots
- eczema
- psoriasis
- excessive pallor
- skin diseases

Headaches and migraines
Headaches are one of our most common afflictions. Millions of people seek medical help for this problem every year, and millions of pounds are spent on headache remedies annually.

Most headaches are caused not by disease but by fatigue, emotional disorders, or allergies.

Intermittent tension headaches are caused by worry, anxiety, overwork, or inadequate ventilation. The most common type – a chronic tension headache – is often caused by depression. Brain tissue itself is insensitive to pain, as is the bony covering of the brain (the cranium). Headache pain results from the stimulation of such pain-sensitive structures as the membranous linings of the brain (the meninges) and the nerves of the cranium and upper neck. This stimulation can be produced by inflammation, by the dilation of blood vessels of the head, or by muscle spasms in the neck and head. Headaches brought on by muscle spasms are classified as tension headaches; those caused by the dilation of blood vessels are called vascular headaches.

Almost 90 per cent of all persons seeking medical help for headaches suffer from tension headaches. These are characterised by a diffuse ache that either spreads over the entire head or feels like a tight headband. Tension headaches are often usually associated with poor sleep and persistent tension in the muscles of the neck, shoulders and forehead. These muscles must relax before the pain eases.

Migraine is the most common from of vascular headache. About 60 per cent of all migraine sufferers are women, and most sufferers first develop symptoms between the ages of 10 and 30. In approximately 30 per cent of all cases, migraine attacks are preceded by warning signs such as blind spots, zigzag flashing lights, numbness in parts of the body, and distorted visual images. Migraine pain almost always occurs on only one side and is usually accompanied by nausea. Many things seem capable of triggering migraine attacks, including stress, fatigue, changes in the weather, fasting, menstruation, drugs, such as birth control pills, that contain oestrogen, and foods, such as cheese, alcohol, and chocolate, that contain substances that affect the blood vessels. Many migraine patients have family histories of the problem.

Many of the relaxation techniques and alternative therapies outlined later in this book will help to alleviate headaches. However, chronic headaches may be physical symptoms of depression or other kinds of severe emotional problems. If you suffer from persistent headaches, then be sure to consult your doctor for professional treatment.

Premenstrual Syndrome (PMS)
Stress has a debilitating effect on the nerves in general, and certain premenstrual symptoms may be aggravated by stress. Many sufferers of PMS have abnormal levels of the adrenal hormone aldosterone, which may account for some of the problems of excessive fluid retention and weight gain, breast tenderness and abdominal bloating. Further release of aldosterone caused by stress will exacerbate these problems.

Depression
Chronic stress can produce severe depression, because of its debilitating psychological effects. The physiological changes produced by stress can also contribute to depression. Adrenaline

and noradrenaline are not only adrenal hormones but also chemical messengers in the brain. Deficiencies of noradrenaline have been linked to depression in certain individuals, and so adrenal exhaustion through chronic long-term stress may be a contributory factor in depressive illness.

PART TWO

The Causes of Stress

Environmental stress

Urban decay and deprivation are a major source of distress for large sections of the population. Inadequate housing, noise, pollution, crowding, violence and poverty create some of the most cumulative and pervasive forms of stress. These factors affect how we live, work and play. Their impact depends on the infrastructure of the location, transport requirements, and availability of opportunities to spend time away from the environment.

Light

The nature of light is an essential factor in

the quality of our lives. Natural light is as vital for healthy living as the air we breathe. It regulates levels of the hormone melatonin, which influences sleep, mood and the reproductive cycle. Our instinctive love of light and the sun explains our annual migration to hotter climates.

A lack of daylight can induce an accumulation of melatonin, creating lethargy and depression. The syndrome Seasonal Adaptive Depression (SAD), which is a pattern of depressive illness in which symptoms recur every winter, afflicts large numbers of people. Sufferers feel antisocial, tired and depressed. Photo-therapy – morning exposure to bright, full-spectrum light – can often be dramatically helpful in treating SAD sufferers. In general, it is usually more healthy to work beside windows and let as much daylight into the home as possible. Fluorescent lighting, the most unnatural form of light, should be avoided where possible, but as artificial light is a necessary evil it is best to use full-spectrum lights that simulate daylight.

Colour

Colour affects many aspects of our lives and can have a significant effect on our moods and perceptions. We are all colour biased – we may chose colour as a response to their innate properties or we may just have a distinctive preference for it. Colours have physical as well as psychological effects. Research has shown that physiological responses such as blood pressure and brain-wave patterns vary according to which colour we are being exposed to. For example, exposure to red, the most stimulating colour, can lead to an increase of blood pressure while exposure to blue light has the opposite effect.

Life events and the pace of change

In the following table of stressful events, compiled by two American doctors, T. H. Holmes and R. H. Rahe (*Journal of Psychosomatic Research no 11*, 1967), specific events are weighted on a scale from 0 to 100.

The chart suggests that it is *change itself* that is stressful – moving house, getting married, redundancy, etc – regardless of whether the change is regarded as favourable or unfavourable. Scores of about 300 supposedly indicate a major life crisis, scores of 200 to 299 a moderate life crisis, and 100 to 199 a mild life crisis.

Event	Life Change Units
Death of a spouse	100
Divorce	73
Marital separation	65
Imprisonment	63
Death of a close relation	63
Personal injury or illness	53
Marriage/engagement/cohabitation	50
Loss of job	47
Marital reconciliation	45
Retirement	45
Illness in the family	44
Pregnancy	44
Sexual problems	39
Birth of a child	39
Business readjustment	39
Change in financial state	38

Death of a close friend	37
Change to a different type of work	36
Large mortgage or loan	31
Foreclosure of mortgage or loan	31
Change in job responsibilities	29
Son or daughter leaving home	29
Outstanding personal achievement	28
Beginning or end of school or college	26
Change in living conditions	25
Change in personal habits (more or less exercise)	24
Trouble with the boss	23
Change in working hours or conditions	20
Moving house	20
Change of school or college	20
Change in recreation	19
Change in social activities	18
Change in sleeping habits	16
Holiday	13
Christmas	12
Minor violations of the law	11

Personal relationships

The quality of personal relationships is tradition-ally regarded as one of the main sources of stress. The relationship between partners is the key fac-tor, followed by the parent–child relationship. Factors that contribute to successful and relatively stress-free relationships include:

- communication
- honesty with yourself and partner
- listening
- respect for yourself and partner
- realistic expectations
- quality time together
- quality time apart

Home and family

Many sources of stress, such as bereavement, financial worries and relationship breakdowns, which feature prominently in the Holmes and Rahe scale, originate within the family.

Increases in stress over the last 30 years can be partly explained by changing social factors. Within the context of a large extended family, and a close working and social environment, an individual benefits from contact and communication with others, receives feedback to establish realistic life goals and meaning, as well as useful information and practical help to overcome problems. The dissolution of these close social support networks makes the individual more vulnerable to various stress-related chronic illnesses.

In the same period it has also become clear that, as well as being a source of support, affection and love, the home can also be the place where individuals, especially women and children, are most likely to suffer varying degrees of physical and emotional abuse.

Parenthood

Parenthood imposes heavy physical, emotional and financial burdens, which can crush the less resilient. Combining childcare and full-time employment is the most stressful of all, especially for the working mother, who is more likely to be responsible for a bigger share of the housework and childcare than the father. In this situation, arguments, disagreements, misunderstandings, resentments and depression are more likely to surface. The following advice can help to reduce parental stress levels:

- care for yourself as well as the children

- keep a sense of self, apart from the role of parent

- plan, prepare and prioritise to exploit free time

- use free time in a creative and stimulating way

- partners should acknowledge and define shared responsibilities

- preserve healthy communication

- avoid self recrimination – no one is perfect

- be prepared to use family, friends and agencies for support

Stress at work

Work provides an income and also fulfils a variety of other human needs – mental and physical exercise, social contact, a feeling of self-worth and competence. Work, however, is also a major source of stress, arising from the nature of the relations between management and employees, and that between colleagues in the workplace in general.

The drive for success

Western society is driven by the work ethic. We are taught at a very early age to equate personal adequacy with professional success, making us crave status and abhor failure. Our culture demands a monetary success together with professional identity, and it takes a strong personality to step off the ladder.

Changing work patterns

In our post-industrial society's climate of increasing unemployment and greater leisure time, many people feel lucky to have a job at all. Unemployment, redundancy, a shorter working week and the impact of new technology are affecting our physical and emotional security. Careers for life are no longer guaranteed, and more employers offer short-term contracts that preclude them from offering sickness or holiday pay. Financial and emotional burnout is therefore increasingly common among all levels of the workforce.

Working conditions
There can be little doubt that an individual's physical and mental health is adversely affected by unpleasant working conditions – such as high noise levels, too much or too little lighting, extremes of temperature, and unsocial or excessive hours.

Overwork
An individual may experience stress through an inability to cope with the technical or intellectual demands of a particular task. On the other hand, no matter how competent you are at your job, circumstances, such as long hours, unreal-

istic deadlines, and frequent interruptions, will all produce stress.

Underwork
An employee may experience boredom because there is not enough to do, or because a particular job is dull and repetitive.

Uncertainty
Uncertainty about an individual's work role – work objectives, responsibilities, and colleagues' expectations – and a lack of communication and feedback can result in confusion, frustration, helplessness, and stress.

Conflict
Stress may arise from work that an individual does not want to do or that conflicts with their personal, social and family values.

Responsibility
The greater the level of responsibility the greater the level of stress.

Relationships at work
Good relationships at work with superiors, sub-
ordinates and colleagues are crucial. Within an
organisation, open discussion of problems is essential to encourage positive relationships.

Change at work
Changes that alter psychological, physiological
and behavioural routines, such as promotion, re-
tirement and redundancy, are extremely stressful.

Working conditions survey
CAUSES
3 points each
❑ company has been taken over recently

❑ staff reductions/layoffs in the past year

❑ department/company had major reorganisa-
    tion

❑ staff expect company to be sold or relocated

❑ employee benefits significantly cut recently

Understanding Stress

❏ mandatory overtime frequently required

❏ employees have little control over their work

❏ consequences of making mistakes are severe

❏ workloads vary greatly

❏ most work is machine-paced or fast-paced

❏ staff must react quickly and accurately to change

2 points each

❏ few chances of opportunities for advancement

❏ red tape hinders getting things done

❏ inadequate staffing, money or technology

❏ pay is below the going rate

❏ sick and holiday benefits are below the norm

❏ employees are rotated between shifts

❏ new machines/work methods have been introduced

❏ noise/vibration levels are high or temperature keeps changing

❏ employees normally isolated from one another

❏ performance of work units normally below average

REMEDIES
3 points each

❏ staff recognised and rewarded for their contributions

❏ management takes firm action to reduce stress

❏ mental health benefits are provided

❏ company has formal employee communications programme

❏ staff given information on coping with stress

❏ staff given clear job descriptions

❏ management and staff talk openly with one another

❏ employees are free to talk with one another

2 points each

❑ work rules are published and are the same for everyone

❑ child care programmes are available

❑ employees can work flexible hours

❑ perks are granted fairly

❑ employees have access to necessary technology

❑ staff and management are trained in resolving conflicts

❑ staff receive training when assigned new tasks

❑ company encourages work and personal support groups

❑ staff have space and time for relaxation

1 point each

❑ staff assistance programme is available

❑ each employee's work space is not crowded

❑ staff can have personal items in their work areas

❑ management appreciates humour in the workplace

❑ programmes for care of the elderly are available

Subtract the total points for stress reducers from
the total for stress producers. Results will range
from minus 50 for excellent working conditions,
to plus 60 points for a very stressful working
environment.

Personality traits
Type-A and Type-B personalities
Two American cardiologists, Friedmann and
Rosenman, noticed that many of their patients
with heart disease shared similar personality characteristics and tended to find it difficult to adjust
their lifestyle in a way that would aid recupera-
tion. After detailed research they discovered a significant relationship between certain habitual behavioural patterns and stress-related illness. They
reported that males with Type-A behaviour were
six times as likely to suffer heart disease as men

who exhibited Type-B behaviour. Type-A behaviour features four main patterns:

- *intense sense of time urgency* – always rushed, trying to achieve more in less time

- *inappropriate hostility and aggression* – excessively competitive, finds it difficult to relax and have fun; slight provocation may trigger hostility

- *multiple behaviour* – engages in two or more things simultaneously at improper times

- *lack of proper planning* – lack of planning to achieve required goals

Many studies of people who exhibit Type-A personalities in a wide range of contexts show that common characteristics include:

- work longer hours

- spend more time in classes (students)

- travel more for business

- get less sleep

- more involved in voluntary work, clubs, etc

- spend less time resting or relaxing

- work more around the home

- communicate less with their partners

- less marital sex

- derive little pleasure from socialising

Type-A behaviour places more stress on the cardiovascular system, stimulating high blood pressure, high heart rate and increased risk of heart attacks.

Type-B behaviour is the opposite: more relaxed, less hurried, less competitive. The main character traits include:

- *able to take the long view* – they don't try to meet unrealistic targets or to take on more than they can cope with; better at delegating

- *speed is not that important* – don't worry if not every task can be completed to deadline

- *sense of personal identity* – don't feel they

have to earn respect and love; secure in who they are and what they do

- *sense of proportion* – no sense of constant struggle; always maintain a sense of balance at events in their lives

Classifying individuals as either Type-A or Type-B personalities helps to explain why some people are more prone to stress-related disease. It should be emphasised, however, that the distinction between these two personality types is not absolute; most people will fall between the two extreme types described.

Personality Type Questionnaire

In the list of attributes on page 57, circle the number that most closely represents your own behaviour.

At one end of the scale is Type-A behaviour, the other is Type-B behaviour. High Type-A scores are obtained on the right side of the scale for questions 2, 5, 7, 11, 13, 14; High Type-A scores are obtained on the left side of the scale

	Scale		
1 Never late	1 2 3 4 5 0 4 3 2 1	Casual about appointments
2 Not competitive	1 2 3 4 5 0 4 3 2 1	Very competitive
3 Anticipates what others are going to say (nods; interrupts, finishes for them)	1 2 3 4 5 0 4 3 2 1	Good listener
4 Always rushed	1 2 3 4 5 0 4 3 2 1	Never feels rushed
5 Can wait patiently	1 2 3 4 5 0 4 3 2 1	Impatient while waiting
6 Goes all out	1 2 3 4 5 0 4 3 2 1	Casual
7 Takes things one at a time	1 2 3 4 5 0 4 3 2 1	Tries to do too much
8 Emphatic in speech	1 2 3 4 5 0 4 3 2 1	Slow, deliberate talker
9 Wants good job recognised by others	1 2 3 4 5 0 4 3 2 1	Seeks self-satisfaction regardless of others
10 Fast (eating, walking, etc)	1 2 3 4 5 0 4 3 2 1	Slow doing things
11 Easy-going	1 2 3 4 5 0 4 3 2 1	Hard-driving
12 Hides feelings	1 2 3 4 5 0 4 3 2 1	Expresses feelings
13 Many outside interests	1 2 3 4 5 0 4 3 2 1	Few outside interests
14 Satisfied with job	1 2 3 4 5 0 4 3 2 1	Ambitious

for questions 1, 3, 4, 6, 8, 9, 10, 12. Give your-self 10 points if you score at the end of the scale towards Type-A, working down to 0 points at the other end of the scale, which represents Type-B.

Childhood influences and upbringing
A traumatic childhood is likely to lead to greater levels of stress as an adult. A difficult childhood is also more likely to lead to low self-esteem, low self-assertiveness, difficulty expressing personal beliefs, attitudes and feelings, and a tendency to depend on others to provide a sense of emotional wellbeing and self-worth. Overdependence upon others is likely to lead to frustration as expectations are inevitably dashed – leading to feelings of frustration, anger, depression and hopelessness in adulthood.

Unrealistic expectations
Unrealistic expectations are a common source of stress. People often become upset about something, not because it is innately stressful

but because it does not concur with what they expected. Take, for example, the experience of driving in slow-moving traffic. If it happens at rush hour, you may not like it but it should not surprise or upset you. However, if it occurs on a Sunday afternoon, especially if it makes you late for something, you are more likely to be stressed by it.

When expectations are realistic, life feels more predictable and therefore more manageable. There is an increased feeling of control because you can plan and prepare yourself (physically and psychologically). For example, if you know in advance when you have to work overtime or stay late, you will take it more in your stride than when it is dropped on you at the last minute.

Attitudes and beliefs
A lot of stress results from our beliefs. We have literally thousands of premises and assumptions about all kinds of things that we hold to be the truth – everything from, 'You can't beat the sys-

tem' and 'The customer is always right', to 'Men shouldn't show their emotions' and 'Children should tidy their rooms'. We have beliefs about how things are, how people should behave and about ourselves ('I can never remember people's names'). Most of our beliefs are held unconsciously so we are unaware of them. This gives them more power over us and allows them to run our lives.

Beliefs cause stress in two ways. The first is the behaviour that results from them. For example, if you believe that work should come before pleasure, you are likely to work harder and have less leisure time than you would otherwise. If you believe that people should meet the needs of others before they meet their own, you are likely to neglect yourself to some extent. These beliefs are expressions of a personal philosophy or value system, which results in increased effort and decreased relaxation – a formula for stress. There is no objective truth to begin with. These are really just opinions but they lead to stressful behaviour. Uncovering the unconscious assumptions behind actions can be helpful in changing one's lifestyle.

The second way in which beliefs cause stress is when they are in conflict with those of other people. However, it should always be remembered that personal assumptions are not the truth but rather opinions and, therefore, they can be challenged. In situations of conflict it is always helpful if the protagonists attempt to revise their beliefs, or at least admit that the beliefs held by the other person may be just as valid as their own. This mind-opening exercise usually helps to diminish stressful antagonism.

PART THREE

Self Help

It would not be possible, or desirable, to eliminate all the effects of stress in our lives. The aim of stress management should be to harness and control the effects of stress to help to enrich our physical, mental and emotional wellbeing. Positive stress management involves recognising the existence and type of stress and then taking remedial action.

By getting to the root causes of your stress, you can not only relieve current problems and symptoms, but you can also prevent recurrences.

Remedial action falls into three main categories:

- change your thinking

- change your behaviour

- change your lifestyle

Change your thinking
Reframing
Reframing is one of the most powerful and creative stress reducers. It is a technique used to
change the way you look at things in order to
feel better about them. We all do this inadvert-
ently at times. The key to reframing is to recognise that there are many ways to interpret the
same situation. It is like the age-old question: Is
the glass half empty or half full? The answer of
course is that it is both or either, depending on
your point of view. However, if you see the glass
as half full, it will feel different than seeing it as
half empty because the way we feel almost always results from the way we think. The message of reframing is this: there are many ways
of seeing the same thing – so you might as well
pick the one you like. Reframing does not

Your Rights

1. I have the right to express my feelings.
2. I have the right to express my opinions and beliefs.
3. I have the right to say 'Yes' and 'No' for myself.
4. I have the right to change my mind.
5. I have the right to say 'I don't understand'.
6. I have the right simply to be myself, and not act for the benefit of others.
7. I have the right to decline responsibility for other people's problems.
8. I have the right to make reasonable requests of others.
9. I have the right to set my own priorities.
10. I have the right to be listened to, and taken seriously.

Any of the above can be personalised: if your boss asks you to work late at short notice, then by rights 3 and 7, your decision may be: 'I have the right to refuse this unreasonable request, I should have been given more warning'.

change the external reality, but simply helps you to view things differently – and less stressfully.

Positive thinking

When faced with stressful situations try to avoid becoming preoccupied with debilitating negative thoughts of powerlessness, dejection, failure and despair. Chronic stress can leave us vulnerable to negative suggestion, so try to focus on positives:

- focus on your strengths
- learn from the stress you are under
- look for opportunities in the stressful situation
- seek out the positive – make a change

Change your behaviour
Be assertive

Being assertive means taking control and advancing your own needs and aspirations whilst remaining aware of the wishes of others. Assertiveness helps to manage stressful situations, and will in time help to reduce their frequency. Lack of assertiveness is often a function of low self-esteem and low self-confidence, factors that aggravate stress levels and can turn even relatively benign situations and events into potential crises.

The key to assertiveness is verbal and non-verbal communication. People who cannot adequately communicate their needs or wishes will create various problems for themselves. For example, the person who cannot say 'no' to others' requests is likely to be overwhelmed by external demands; the person who finds it difficult to express personal feelings and thoughts will lack self-fulfilment and not be comfortable with his or her own identity; an overly aggressive style of communication will prevent an individual from forming close personal relationships.

We all display different degrees of passive, aggressive or assertive behaviour, at different times and in different situations. Problems arise when a particular response is unhelpful for a particular situation, and we find it difficult to change to a more appropriate style of response. Improving assertiveness is about learning how to extend the range of our communication style to allow a greater flexibility of responses in different situations.

It is important to acknowledge that we are all equal and have the same basic rights (*see* page 64). Being too passive means denying one's rights by failing to express honest feelings, thoughts and beliefs, and allowing others to violate oneself. A passive person may express thoughts and feelings in such an apologetic, self-effacing manner that others can easily disregard them. Being non-assertive means allowing people to walk all over you, denying the validity of your own needs, and surrendering control over a situation to others. This leads to stressful feelings of anxiety, powerlessness, frustration and anger.

Being assertive involves standing up for your personal rights and expressing your thoughts, feelings and beliefs directly, honestly and spontaneously in ways that don't infringe the rights of others. Assertive people respect themselves and others, and take responsibility for their actions and choices. They recognise their needs and ask openly and directly for what they want. If they fail in these efforts, for whatever reason, they may feel disappointed, but their self-confidence remains intact. They are not reliant on the approval of others.

Useful verbal and nonverbal assertive skills include the ability to:

- Establish good eye contact, but do not stare.

- Stand or sit comfortably without fidgeting.

- Talk in a firm steady voice instead of rambling or shouting.

- Use gesture to emphasise points (hands, facial expressions, body posture).

- Use statements such as 'I think', 'I feel'.

- Use empathetic statements of interest such as 'What do you think', 'How do you feel?'

- Be concise and to the point. State clearly the message you want the other person to hear.

The more you stand up for yourself the higher your self-esteem. Your chances of getting what you want out of life improve greatly when you let others know what you want and you stand up for your own rights and needs. Expressing negative feelings at the appropriate time avoids the buildup of resentment. Being less self-conscious and anxious, and less driven by the need for self-protection and control, you will be able to manage stress more successfully, and to love and appreciate yourself and others more easily.

Get organised
Being chronically disorganised, either at work or in the home, is one of the most common causes of stress. Stressful environments are minimised when you impose a form of struc-

ture: this offers security against problems appearing 'out-of-the-blue'. Too inflexible a pattern would be impractical, but keeping a diary, writing lists and prioritising duties all help to stem stressful situations. Writing down objectives, duties and activities helps to make them seem more tangible and surmountable. Don't try to overload your mind with too much information – if you are already stressed there is more chance of you forgetting vital references and data. If you keep control over what you are doing there is less chance of spiralling into professional and personal chaos.

Ventilation

There is an old saying that 'a problem shared is a problem halved'. People who keep things to themselves carry a considerable and unnecessary burden. Talking through a problem with others can be the first step to eliminating it. It is worth developing a support system – a few trusted relatives, colleagues or friends to talk to when you are upset or worried. Often it's not events themselves that are stressful but how we perceive them. Another form of communication that may be helpful is writing, for example in a private journal at home, or even letters to one-self, which should then be destroyed. The value is in expressing the feelings and getting them out. Rereading the letter just reinforces the up-set and reawakens the anger.

Record your emotions
Keeping a work diary will help you to stay or-ganised. Keeping a personal journal will help you to express your emotions and understand them better. Keeping a daily record, in chart form, of your emotions and stress levels can also help you to identify the stressful aspects of your life. Making a record of this informa-tion, even just for a week, may show that the same kinds of stressful situations recur again and again. Recognising what they are is the first step towards fighting the stress. The chart may soon show that a combination of reorganisation, lifestyle and attitude change and relaxation tech-

Sample emotion chart

Day	Time	Situation	Person
Mon	8.40 am	Heavy traffic	—
	9.10 am	Late for work	—
	11 am	Dealt with complaint. My mistake.	Angry, shouting customer
	2 pm	Cancellation of date by friend	Sharon
	3 pm	Praised in meeting	Mr Smith (boss)
	4.55 pm	Computer crashes and I lose 1 hour's work	—
	7 pm	Argument about household chores	Peter (son)
	9 pm	Time to relax and talk	Eric (husband)
Tues	8 am	Roadworks	—
	8.50 am	Re-did the work I lost last night	—
	10 am	Workmate trying to shift her workload on to me	Patricia

Emotion	Stress level	Avoidance tactics
Frustration	Moderate	Take new route
Worry	Moderate to high	Leave earlier
Restrained anger	High	Organise records better
Disappointment, annoyance	Moderate	Do not dwell on disappointment
Happy, relieved	Low	—
Frustration, anger at self	High	Save work regularly and back up
Annoyance	High	Start chores rota? Avoid shouting, but be firm.
Calm, happy	None	—
Irritated	Slight	Kept reminding myself that I had lots of time
Slightly annoyed	Low	—
Very annoyed	High	Arrange meeting to discuss business schedule

niques may be required. The aim is to encourage you yourself to devise ways of avoiding or coping with difficult situations. An example of such a chart is given on pages 72 and 73.

Humour
Humour is a wonderful stress-reducer and antidote to upsets, both at home and at work; we often laugh hardest when we have been feeling most tense. Laughter relieves muscular tension, improves breathing, regulates the heart beat and pumps endorphins – the body's natural painkillers – into the bloodstream.

Diversion and distraction
Take time out (anything from a short walk to a holiday) to get away from the things that are bothering you. This will not resolve the problem, but it gives you a break and a chance for your stress levels to decrease. Then, you can return to deal with issues feeling more rested and in a better frame of mind.

Change your lifestyle
Diet

Most experts agree that a well-balanced diet is crucial in preserving health and helping to reduce stress. Certain foods and drinks act as quite powerful stimulants to the body and so are a direct cause of stress. This stimulation may be pleasurable in the short term, but more harmful with prolonged consumption.

Caffeine

Caffeine is a drug commonly found in food and drinks such as coffee, tea, chocolate and Coca-Cola. It is a strong stimulant that actually generates a stress reaction in the body by causing a rise in the release of adrenaline. In small doses caffeine can have a positive effect on our health – its initial effects are increased alertness, and increased activity in the muscles, nervous system and heart. But too much caffeine has the same effect on the systems as prolonged stress: lethargy, anxiety, over-stimulation, headaches, migraine, emotional instability and palpitations. People often use caffeine to fuel an already overloaded system. Some studies have also indicated a possible link between caffeine intake and high blood pressure and high cholesterol levels.

The best way to observe the effect of caffeine is to get it out of the system long enough to see if there is a difference in how you feel. After about three weeks many people notice a benefit. You feel more relaxed, less jittery or nervous, sleep better, have more energy (a paradox, since you are removing a stimulant), less heartburn and fewer muscle aches. To avoid withdrawal symptoms it is best to decrease intake by one drink per day until they you are down to zero, then abstain for three weeks.

Alcohol

Alcohol is another very popular drug. Evidence suggests that moderate alcohol consumption may lessen the risks of heart disease, but when used to excess it has many debilitating consequences for physical and mental health. In terms of stress it has a number of important effects.

Like caffeine, alcohol stimulates the secretion of adrenaline, producing the same problems of nervous tension, irritability and insomnia. Alcohol in excess will increase fat deposits in the heart and decrease immune function. Alcohol is also a toxin to the bone marrow, and has a severe impact on the liver, inhibiting that organ's ability to detoxify the body. These toxins include hormones released during stress, which will continue to circulate in the body if liver function is impaired.

Smoking

Many people use cigarettes as a coping mechanism in times of stress, and it seems that smoking can help to reduce stress in the short term. The long-term hazards of smoking, however, far outweigh its palliative properties. Smoking is one of the major causes of illness and death worldwide. Cigarettes unquestionably cause a variety of cancers, especially of the lung and bladder, and also contribute to the development of hypertension, respiratory illness and heart disease.

Sugar

Simple sugar contains none of the essential nutrients, such as protein, fibre, minerals or vitamins. Excess consumption of sugar results in a short-term surge of energy through the body, leading to the possible exhaustion of the adrenal glands. This can result in irritability, poor concentration and depression. High sugar intake can also result in jumps in blood sugar, placing stress on the pancreas, which produces insulin, resulting in a greater risk of developing diabetes (*see* page 30). Excessive sugar consumption can also lead to a variety of unpleasant health problems, including severe tooth decay, obesity, emotional instability and hypoglycaemia.

Sugar consumption can be reduced by eating fresh fruit for dessert instead of sugary puddings; drinking unsweetened fruit juices and sugar-free squashes and carbonated drinks; leaving out sugar in coffee and tea; looking for sugar-free labels on products in supermarkets; and avoiding junk foods.

Salt
Salt should be minimised in your diet. Foods high in salt, such as refined convenience foods, bacon, ham, sausages and pickled items, should be avoided. Excessive intake of salt can have a variety of harmful side effects, such as increased blood pressure, depletion of the adrenal glands, and emotional instability. Instead of salt use a salt substitute that is rich in potassium rather than in sodium.

Fat
It is important to limit the amount of fat in our diet. Too much fat causes obesity and puts unnecessary strain on the heart. There is also evidence that high-fat diets contribute to the growing incidence of breast, colon and prostate cancers in Western society. There are basically two types of fat:

- *saturated fats* – in milk, cheese, butter, animal fats, vegetable fats, biscuits, cakes and sweets

- *unsaturated fats* – which include *polyunsaturated fats* found in sunflower oil, corn oil, soya oil, nuts, trout, mackerel and herring.

Nutritionists advise that we should substitute polyunsaturated fats for saturated fats wherever possible. This will help to avoid the tendency towards obesity and raised cholesterol levels in the blood, which can lead to cardiovascular disease and premature death.

Healthy eating

It should be clear by now that it is important to avoid too much salt, sugar and dairy products in our diet. These foods tend to promote adrenaline release, which decreases stress tolerance, and they also have a negative effect on cardiovascular health. As part of a balanced diet, the following foods will encourage fitness and energy, nourish nerves, feed muscles, improve circulation and breathing, support the immune system and promote a general feeling of positivity and calm:

- *whole grains* – wheat, rice, oats, barley, rye, corn – are a source of complex carbohydrates and essential vitamins and minerals and other nutrients that are of great value in improving stress tolerance

- *beans* – soybeans, kidney beans, broad beans, lentils, chick peas – are an excellent source of anti-stress B-vitamins

- *fresh fruit and vegetables* – are an excellent source of essential vitamins and dietary fibre

Vitamins and minerals

Vitamins are a group of chemically unrelated, organic nutrients that are essential in small quantities for normal metabolism, growth, and physical wellbeing. These nutrients must be obtained through diet, since they are not synthesised in the body. In general, all the vitamins required by the average person can be obtained from a natural, well-balanced diet. However, stress increases cellular activity, which leads to increased nutrient usage, and under chronic stress certain vitamin deficiencies may occur.

The following vitamins and supplements are available from most chemists and health shops. For more information contact your doctor, local health shop, pharmacist or alternative health practitioner.

Vitamin C

Vitamin C deficiency is a common problem caused by stress, which hampers the body's ability to create and absorb the vitamin. Vitamin C deficiency has been linked to a range of illnesses and disorders, including scurvy, lethargy and fatigue, a weakened immune system and degenerative diseases such as arthritis and arteriosclerosis. Alcohol and cigarettes are also thought to inhibit the action of vitamin C. Foods rich in vitamin C include fresh fruit and vegetables.

Vitamin B_6

Vitamin B_6 is essential to the health of the nervous system. It is important in maintaining a healthy immune system, and there is evidence that B_6 plays a role in limiting the growth of certain tumours and skin cancers. B_6 relieves a wide variety of PMS symptoms, such as breast tenderness, weight gain (water retention) and irritability. This very important vitamin has also been shown to be helpful in reducing or eliminating symptoms of nervous tremors and epileptic seizures. A lack of B_6 can lead to physical and mental exhaustion, and has been linked to anaemia.

Supplements of vitamin B_6 are recommended when under stress, for morning sickness during pregnancy, and for anxiety. Foods rich in vitamin B_6 are fish, fresh vegetables, pulses and whole grain cereals.

Vitamin B_{12}
Vitamin B_{12} is vital for blood formation and a healthy nervous system. Living with persistent and unmanaged stress can and will eventually result in symptoms of physical deterioration and

mental and emotional breakdown. B_{12} helps you to fight disease, recover more quickly from viral infections and helps to restore a sluggish appetite. Foods rich in B_{12} are red meats, fish and dairy products.

VITAMIN B_5 (PANTOTHENIC ACID)
Pantothenic acid is essential for the proper functioning of the adrenal glands, the health of which is so important to the management of stress. Most experts agree that pantothenic acid supplements are recommended to help to alleviate the symptoms of chronic stress.

SELENIUM
This trace element is essential for normal growth and development. It acts as an antioxidant, an anti-polluting agent and helps to strengthen the immune system. Research indicates a possible a link between heart disease and selenium deficiency. Nutritionists advise that selenium supplements are best taken together with vitamin E.

IRON

Iron deficiency leads to tiredness and exhaustion, anaemia and moods of depression. A deficiency in iron can result from vitamin C deficiency, which limits the absorption of iron in the body. Symptoms of iron deficiency include brittle nails, paleness and mouth ulcers. Foods rich in iron include pulses, grains, fish, poultry, meat, spinach, potatoes and peas.

ZINC

Zinc deficiency is a common sign of stress, and can cause stomach problems, a breakdown of the immune system, poor healing, low appetite and fatigue. Foods rich in zinc include seafood, dairy products, meat, ginger root and soya beans.

IODINE

The body's supply of iodine is dependent on a healthy thyroid gland, which determines the metabolic rate of the body – so a deficiency can cause exhaustion, whilst iodine supplements have a stimulant effect. Foods rich in iodine include seafoods, spinach and green peppers.

CALCIUM

Calcium is essential for healthy bones, joints, teeth, nerves, muscles and for efficient blood clotting. Foods rich in calcium include dairy products, pulses, apples and cabbage. Some foods, such as bread and milk, have added calcium and are advertised as calcium-fortified.

Exercise

It is impossible to overestimate the importance of exercise in managing stress. The stress reaction encourages a state of high energy but there is usually no place for that energy to go; therefore, our bodies can stay in a state of arousal for hours at a time. Exercise is the most logical way to dissipate this excess energy. It is what our bodies are trying to do when we pace around or tap our legs and fingers. It is much better to channel it into a more complete form of exercise like a brisk walk, a run, a bike ride or a game of squash. During times of high stress, we could benefit from an immediate physical outlet – but this often is not possible. However, regular ex-

How Exercise Reduces Stress

1. Muscular relaxation and exercise reduce muscle tension. They use up the energy released by the 'fight-or-flight' response.
2. Prolonged aerobic exercise causes production of endorphins, which produce feelings of euphoria and relaxation.
3. Exercise improves and maintains good circulation and lowers blood pressure.
4. Exercise may help to clear the mind of worrying thoughts and anxieties and can encourage more creativity and problem solving.
5. Exercise improves self-image and appearance and helps to control weight.
6. Exercise may result in increased social contact and also provides a balance with other activities, e.g. work/school, home and family responsibilities.

ercise can drain off ongoing stress and keep things under control: it improves sleep, reduces headaches, creates a feeling of wellbeing, helps concentration and increases stamina. Chemicals called endorphins are released into the brain during exercise. Morphine-like in their effect, these substances promote a sense of positivity and happiness, which will last for some time after exercising.

At the very least, it is important to exercise three times per week for a minimum of 30 minutes each time. Aerobic activities like walking, jogging, swimming, cycling, squash, skiing, aerobics classes and dancing are suitable. Choose things you like to do or they will feel like a chore and you will begin to avoid them. It is important not to push yourself too hard in the beginning, and to seek medical advice on which form of sport to take up. The body benefits more from short periods of regular exercise rather than infrequent bursts. Ease yourself into an exercise programme, as doing too much too soon could lead to physical exhaustion or injury.

Sleep

As mundane as it sounds, sleep is an important way of reducing stress. Fatigue is a common component of chronic stress (in some cases resulting from stress-induced insomnia), and when tired it is more difficult to cope with stressful situations. These dynamics can create a vicious cycle. When distressed individuals get more sleep, they feel better and are more resilient and adaptable in dealing with day-to-day events.

Most people know what their usual sleep requirement is (the range is five to ten hours per night; the average being seven to eight), but a surprisingly large percentage of the population is chronically sleep-deprived. If you do feel constantly tired, go to bed 30 to 60 minutes earlier and monitor the results after a few days or a week. If you are still tired, go to bed 30 minutes earlier than this. Eventually, there will be a pattern which does help to reduce stress. The three criteria of success are:

• waking refreshed

- plenty of daytime energy

- waking naturally before the alarm goes off

Sleeping-in is fine, but if you sleep too long, it throws off your body rhythms during the following day. It is better to go to bed earlier.

Daytime naps are an interesting phenomenon. They can be valuable if they are short and timed properly (i.e. not in the evening). The catnap is a short sleep (five to 20 minutes) that can be rejuvenating. A nap lasting more than 30 minutes can make you feel groggy. If you suffer with insomnia daytime naps are not a good idea. Beyond these cautionary notes, getting more sleep can be important in reducing stress and helping you to cope and function better.

Leisure

No one would expect a tennis player to complete an entire match without taking breaks. Surprisingly though, many otherwise rational people think nothing of working from dawn to dusk without taking a break and then wonder why they become distressed.

Pacing

It is important to learn to monitor stress and energy levels, and then pace ourselves accordingly. Pacing is about awareness and vigilance – knowing when to extend ourselves and when to ease up. It is also about acting on the information supplied by our bodies. The graph below illustrates the relationship between stress and performance, and leads to the following important conclusions:

- Increased stress produces increased performance, initially.

- Once you pass a certain point (the hump), any more stress results in decreased performance. Trying harder at this point is unproductive or even counterproductive. The only sensible option is to take a break.

- We need a certain amount of stress to function well. However, stress becomes harmful

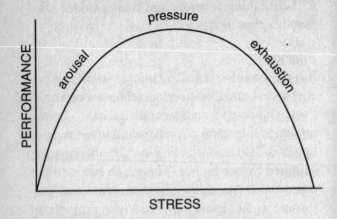

when there is too much, when it lasts too long, or when it occurs too often.

- One of the first symptoms of distress is fatigue, which we tend to ignore. It is a good idea to take steps to reduce stress levels at this point, before fatigue becomes exhaustion.

The other key to pacing is taking periodic rest. Too many people go far too long without breaks. Just as we all have cycles of deep sleep and dream sleep throughout the night (at roughly 90-

to 120-minute intervals), we also have cycles through the day (peaks of energy and concentration interspersed with troughs of low energy and inefficiency). These cycles are called ultradian rhythms because they happen many times per day (as opposed to the 25-hour circadian rhythm). We need to watch for these troughs and take 20-minute breaks when they occur, as opposed to working through them and building up stress.

It is not always convenient for us to take breaks when nature tells us to, but we can all become better at this. A mid-morning break, lunch, a mid-afternoon break and supper divide the day into roughly two hour segments. These time-outs can include catnaps, meditation, daydreaming, a social interlude, a short walk, a refreshment break, a change to low-concentration tasks, or listening to music. Like the catnap, it is simply a good investment of time that pays itself back quickly in increased productivity and reduced stress.

Work/leisure balance

Optimising the balance between work and leisure is an important means to eliminating unwanted stress in our lives. Despite all our labour-saving devices, leisure is still an elusive commodity for most people. Statistics show that we are working an extra three hours per week compared with 20 years ago. That translates into an extra month of work each year. Add to that the phenomenon of the two career family (which makes family and leisure time even more scarce) and you start to get a picture of society on an accelerating treadmill.

Leisure time and levels of distress are inversely proportional – the less leisure, the more stress. It may be useful to divide your life (excluding sleep time) into four compartments (work, family, community and self) and then to assess what percentage of your time and energy in an average week goes into each part. There is no normal range, but when work is over 60 per cent and/or when self is less than 10 per cent this indicates there may be a problem with stress.

We all require time to meet our own needs (self-care, self-nurturing, etc) and when that is neglected, trouble usually follows. Self-directed activities can include exercise or recreation, relaxation, socialising, entertainment and hobbies.

The word leisure is derived from the Latin word *licere,* which means 'permission'. The main reason so many people do not have enough leisure is that they are not giving themselves permission to make the time to enjoy it. Leisure is one of the most pleasant stress relievers ever invented, and it is strange that people resist it so much.

PART FOUR

Therapy

It may not always be possible to alleviate all the causes and symptoms of stress without professional help. In addition to the family doctor, there is a great variety of various alternative therapies and medicines available, many of which provide excellent stress relief.

Conventional medicine
Tranquillisers
There are a variety of tranquillising drugs that act to suppress the central nervous system, thereby reducing anxiety and other stress-related symptoms. Benzodiazepines, such as Valium, Librium or Ativan, are the most com-

monly prescribed minor tranquillisers. Because these products have few side effects and are relatively safe in overdose, they have come to replace barbiturates as prescribed sedatives and sleeping pills.

Benzodiazepines depress mental activity and alertness, but do not generally make you drowsy or clumsy as do barbiturates, but they do affect driving and similar skills. Alone, benzodiazepines cannot produce the 'high' that alcohol or barbiturates produce, and after up to two weeks' continuous use, they may become ineffective as sleeping pills, and after four months may become ineffective against anxiety. Long-term dependence is more likely to be psychological; the pills become a means of coping with stressful events, and there may be severe anxiety if the drug is unavailable. Withdrawal symptoms appear in many users if they suddenly stop taking such drugs after about eight years' treatment with normal doses. Symptoms include insomnia, anxiety, tremor, irritability, nausea and vomiting. Such symptoms are more noticeable with shorter-acting benzodiazepines such as lorazepam and temazepam.

In the 1950s and 1960s doctors would prescribe minor tranquillisers almost indiscriminately and for indefinite periods. Nowadays the medical profession is more aware that the short-term benefits of these drugs can be outweighed by long-term problems of dependency and withdrawal. In Britain in 1988, the Committee on Safety of Medicines recommended that minor tranquillisers should be prescribed for a period of no longer than two to four weeks.

Counselling and psychotherapy

There are various support organisations and counselling services available to help with stress management. These range from expensive specialist stress-management experts to free stress clinics run by local doctors. Counselling is especially good for short-term problems: trained experts help you to examine the causes of problems and devise strategies to avoid negative behaviour patterns and restore a sense of physical and emotional wellbeing.

Psychotherapy is used for resolving deeper, long-term emotional and psychological problems. Psychotherapy is usually offered by psychiatrists, clinical psychologists, and psychiatric social workers. Psychiatric social workers are trained in treatment methods and often work as part of a treatment team in hospitals or clinics. Today psychotherapy is being practised more and more by para-professionals, who have less training but may be supervised by a professional or may be trained to work with specific problems using specific methods.

Psychotherapy is conducted in several formats. Individual Therapy refers to a therapist's work with one person on his or her unique problem; the relationship between client and therapist may be particularly important in producing change. In Group Therapy, therapists meet with a group of patients, and the interactions between patients become an important part of the therapy process.

Many different theories or schools of psychotherapy exist. Two of the more common are Psychodynamic Therapy and Behavioural Therapy.

Psychodynamic Therapy makes the fundamental assumption that emotional disorders are merely symptoms of internal, unobservable and unconscious conflicts between personality components. These conflicts result from unresolved family conflicts, experienced in early stages of childhood, that become reactivated in problem situations in adulthood. The aim of psychodynamic therapies is to revive the early conflict and to transfer it to the relationship with the therapist. The symptoms are removed when the therapist helps the patient to resolve the conflict in the transference relationship. The therapist interprets the transference to the patient and helps him or her overcome resistances to accepting the interpretation. Additional methods, such as dream interpretation or word-association techniques, are used to aid in uncovering unconscious material. Sigmund Freud's psychoanalysis is the primary example of a psychodynamic therapy.

Behavioural approaches assume that all behaviour is learned. Emotional disorders are considered to be conditioned responses or habits that can be modified by the same principles of learning that govern all behaviour. From this perspective psychotherapy means providing corrective learning or conditioning experiences. Different therapy techniques are employed for remedying specific disordered behaviours. In social-skills training, for instance, patients practise handling difficult interpersonal situations via role playing.

Relaxation

An effective way to reduce stress in the body is through certain disciplines that fall under the heading of relaxation techniques.

Just as we are all capable of mounting and sustaining a stress reaction, we have also inherited the ability to put our bodies into a state of deep relaxation, called the 'relaxation response'. In this state, all the physiological events in the stress reaction are reversed: the pulse slows down, blood pressure falls, breathing becomes slower, and the muscles relax. But whereas the stress reaction is automatic, the relaxation response has to be deliberately induced. Fortunately, there are many ways of doing this. Sitting quietly in a park or beside the fireplace, gently petting the family cat, reclining on the sofa and other restful activities can generate this state. There also are specific skills that can be learned that are efficient and beneficial.

A state of deep relaxation achieved through meditation or self-hypnosis is actually more physiologically restful than sleep. These techniques are best learned through formal training courses, which are taught in a variety of places. Books and relaxation tapes can be used when courses are not available or are beyond your budget. On days when exercise is not possible, relaxation techniques are an excellent way to bring down the body's stress level. Whereas exercise dissipates stress energy, relaxation techniques neutralise it, producing a calming effect. As little as 20 minutes once or twice per day confers significant benefit.

Planning ahead

Making time in a busy schedule is probably the hardest of all the relaxation criteria to satisfy. You may need to obtain the cooperation of your friends, family or colleagues. If people close to you see you disappearing behind a locked door for twenty minutes or so, they may start wondering... so explain to them what you are doing. You may have to endure a bit of rib-tickling until other people come to appreciate the importance of it to you. If you fail to get support, then you will have to change your itinerary (or your friends).

Choose a time when you are least likely to be disturbed: early morning or late at night, if necessary. You should prepare yourself for relaxation by exercising moderately for five to ten minutes beforehand. You should also exercise moderately for up to three minutes afterwards to help you reorientate. Twenty minutes is the minimum time to spend on this three-part routine.

Get comfortable

It is up to you to ensure that you relax in a completely disturbance-free atmosphere. There must be no radio, no TV, no background music, no incense. Turn on the telephone answering machine and turn down the ringer if it is in the same room. It is best to avoid meals just before relaxation.

Find a comfortable chair in which to sit. Your

back and neck should be straight, your shoulders not hunched forward. Your hands should rest comfortably in your lap half open. Your feet should be on the floor and your legs should not be crossed, just sit naturally. Next make sure there is nothing in the room to distract you, such as insects, draughts, direct sunlight. If you're relaxing in a group do so with experienced people – there's nothing less conducive to relaxation than an outburst of giggles from your flatmate or the person who shares your office.

Loosen off tight clothing like belts, ties and shoe laces. If you must lie down to get comfortable, rest your hands about an inch away from your body either side and don't cross your legs. Physical discomfort of any sort will provoke the secretion of adrenaline to spur you into remedial action, creating a sense of restlessness. Listen to what your body is trying to tell you about avoidable discomfort in your posture and remove the source before you go on.

Correct breathing

Breathing for relaxation should be moderate, slow and rhythmic. Don't hold your breath, and conversely, don't take short gasping breaths. Your whole chest should be involved in breathing – not just the top half – so use both chest and diaphragm muscles. Don't fully inhale or exhale and above all, don't force your breathing, make it natural. Sigh or take deep breaths if you need to – but do try to make it moderate, slow and rhythmic.

Correct attitude

The human mind is a highly complex, mostly automatic processing machine. If you have expectations that are not met, your mind will unconsciously generate a stress response as the first stage in remedying the situation. That stress response will initiate a host of subliminal physiological reactions that make you feel like doing something – the heart rate increases, muscles tense, and a lowering of the body's surface temperature makes you feel uncomfortable. Your attitude, your expectations and your intent are the foundation of your thoughts and your actions. If this foundation is not in keeping with your reality your relaxation will not be complete. Therefore, set your intent on relaxing without expectations and when you get it right it will be a very peaceful, restful and invigorating twenty minutes.

Thought control

Thinking is a form of internalised action, a visualisation of consequences. Through thought we are distinguished from animals who act on instinct alone. However, the mind is an imperfect mirror, and every thought carries with it a kind of charge capable of setting off a stress response before rational decision making can take its turn. For relaxation this is a problem because that thought charge is just as potent as any external stimulus, as anxiety sufferers know only too well.

In order to relax effectively, that is, to reduce the stress response to a minimum for a meaningful period of time, thought has got to be put on hold – you have to stop the internal dialogue.

In the mind there are preconscious entities that float around, dragging you into self-dialogue. Recognising these entities and avoiding their lure is a skill arrived at only with practice, and you must practise this skill every time you relax.

Perseverance

It may look easy to start with, but the benefits of this exercise are mainly long term. Other than noticing an improvement in your ability to sleep at night (or catnap during the day) you may spend many sessions doubting that benefit until you have grown stronger mentally and physically. It is important to persevere – 20 minutes minimum – every day.

Meditation

Meditation is central to the Hindu way of life, and is also an integral part of the other great oriental religions, Buddhism and its close cousin, Zen. It also has its place in Sufism, Christianity and Judaism. (That said, meditation does not require adherence to any of the faiths and religions that advocate it.)

Many people view meditation as peaceful but ineffectual self-centredness. They are wrong: the benefits to be gained from meditation in any of its various forms are many. Those who meditate regularly believe that it leads to a significant lowering of mental tension and negative emotions, while at the same time increasing efficiency at work and deepening the sense of inner calm. This feeling of wellbeing brings physical benefits: regular meditation eliminates or reduces stress; can ease migraine and tension headaches; reduces blood pressure; benefits the heart; and reduces the agony of menstrual cramps.

In its simplest form, meditation is nothing

more than allowing the mind to be lulled by a simple repetitive sensation – waves lapping on the beach, the tinkling of a fountain, repeating a word or sound over and over again, even something as mundane as the sound of machinery, any of these, and countless others, can be used as something on to which the mind focuses so strongly that problems and anxieties are crowded out. In its more refined, mystical guise, it is a means to total self-fulfilment, being completely at one with the universe.

Meditation is neither a time-consuming process – 20 minutes a day are all that is needed – nor is it, as many suspect, a form of self-hypnosis. Practised properly, it is a life-enhancing voyage during which preconceived opinions and ideas fade, the senses and the intellect are refined and the ability to concentrate is increased.

A simple meditation technique
Sit in a comfortable chair, with your feet flat on

the floor, your legs and arms uncrossed. (This can also be done lying down, but you might fall asleep). Rest your hands on your upper legs, with your palms down. Close your eyes, so your mind won't be distracted by what is going on around you.

Direct your focus of awareness to a place six inches (about 20 centimetres) directly above the centre of the top of your head. Here is a location in consciousness which is always calm and radiant, no matter what is going on elsewhere in your mind or body, or around you. It is called the 'upper room'. Think of a point of pure, crystal-white light here. Don't 'try' to visualise it. If you see it, fine, but if you don't, it doesn't matter. As you think of the point of white light, it grows brighter, expanding into a little star, three inches (about 10 centimetres) in diameter.

Think and let the star burn away the veils that have kept it hidden all these years. Direct the star to open, releasing a downpour of cleansing and purifying life energy. This energy is crystal-clear, like fresh spring water.

Let the energy flow through your hair, scalp, into the bones of your head and face, into your brain, eyes, ears, nose, mouth, down the neck, through your shoulders, arms and hands. Experience it flowing through your chest and back, abdomen, hips, pelvic area, upper legs, knees, lower legs, ankles and feet. Think and let the soles of your feet open, releasing the energy into the earth beneath your feet. Now it is flowing through your whole body.

Think of the bottoms of your feet closing, so the energy begins to reflow up through the areas you have cleared out. Experience it in your legs, hips, torso, shoulders, arms, hands, neck and head. Let it overflow out of the top of your head, surrounding your body with an aura of crystal-clear white light.

Bring your hands together, almost but not quite touching, palms facing each other, out in front of your body. Experience the energy flowing through your hands. You could use this energy to heal others, by laying your lighted hands on the person's head, heart, or wherever they have discomfort. Whatever you touch with your hands lighted this way will be filled with inner light-fire-energy.

If you experience discomfort anywhere in your body as you are working with the inner light, think of the 'consuming fire' aspect of the energy. Hold the focus of it in the area of discomfort to burn through the obstructions to the flow of your pure life energy. Afterwards, take a few minutes to assimilate the radiant essence of the light into any area that you have cleared out with the consuming fire aspect.

In addition to your focusing of the energy during meditation, as described above, you can work with the downpour anytime and anywhere, day or night, with your eyes open or closed, as appropriate to the situation. You can use it as an inner shower while you take your outer shower in the morning. Every time you think of the star and the white light downpouring, it continues for about 30 minutes. So you can literally fill your day with inner light. It's also a great way to go to sleep at night. For stress-reduction it is best to practice the technique for at least a few minutes every day.

Massage

We massage ourselves nearly every day; the natural reaction to reach out and touch a painful part of the body – such as a sprain – forms the basis of massage.

The relaxation and healing powers of massage have been well documented over the past 5,000 years. The therapeutic value of applying oils and rubbing parts of the body to lessen pain and prevent illness was recognised amongst the ancient Mediterranean civilisations. In the East it was normal to visit your physician when healthy, and the art of preventative medicine was widely implemented. In ancient times scented oils were almost always used when giving massages, creating an early form of aromatherapy massage. More recently, reflexology, shiatsu and Swedish massage have gained popularity. The aims of these different techniques are basically the same – to relive muscular tension, alleviate fatigue and revive energy.

Massage affects the whole body through rhythmically applied pressure, stroking and pulling. These movements increase blood circulation and cause the blood vessels to dilate. Stimulation of nerves and blood also affects the internal organs. The lymph is a milky white liquid that carries waste substances and toxins away from the tissues via the lymphatic system. The circulation of the lymph is largely dependent on muscle contractions, and so massage will help speed the lymph's progress through the system. Inactivity can cause an unhealthy buildup of the substance. But active people can also benefit from massage – strenuous activity burns up the muscle, producing an increase of waste products in the muscle tissue. Massage will help to balance the system in both cases and can increase oxygen capacity by 10–15 per cent.

Inactive lifestyles and sedentary occupations

have created a society of people with cramped, stooped, and neglected postures. By realigning our bodies, massage can help to repair damaged postures. Not only does massage help to coax the spine and corresponding physiology back into position, it also makes us more aware of our bodies. Relieved of muscle tension, the body feels lighter and can therefore be borne more naturally and with more poise. Used in conjunction with postural therapies such as the Alexander Technique (*see* page 169), massage is a valuable contribution towards a relaxed yet controlled posture.

Many of the benefits of massage come through the healer–patient contact. Our hands are one of the most sensitive parts of our body – we experience much of our sense of touch through our hands. Hand healers are believed to help people through their hands, often without even touching the body. There is a certain element of this in massage techniques. The masseur is communicating feelings of harmony and relaxation through their hands, allowing a benign force to flow into the client. Many practitioners therefore believe that it is important for the masseur to be in a positive state of mind.

A practised masseur will be able to diagnose the patient through touch. They can 'listen' to tension and stress through the texture of the skin, knotted muscles and stiff joints. Old and current sprains, congestion and swelling should all be obvious to a good masseur. The actions of massage – the stroking, kneading and pulling – detoxify the body of these ailments, improving circulation and lymphatic drainage. After these tensions and weaknesses have been pinpointed and relieved, the patient is left feeling relaxed and energised.

Along with the diagnosis element of massage there are great psychological benefits – the enjoyment of touch and of being stroked and caressed by another person. During a massage the patient is coaxed from emotional and occupational stresses and brought into the intense arena of the here and now. Such one-on-one nonverbal communication is a valuable element in our overstressed lifestyles.

Massage – basic techniques

Massage should take place in a comfortably warm room. Use a mid-thigh level table or the floor. You will need a towel and a bottle of oil; vegetable oil will do, but if you wish you can buy a perfumed massage oil from a chemist or health shop, or mix your own using a blend of aromatherapy oils.

EFFLEURAGE (STROKING)
The movement of effleurage is slow and rhyth-

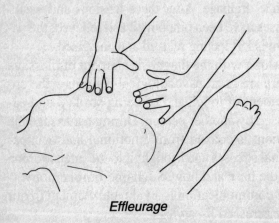

Effleurage

mical, using the whole hand in an upward direction towards the heart. Light, gliding strokes are used when working away from the heart. Applied lightly this has a relaxing effect on the nervous system, whilst stronger pressure has more effect on the blood circulation and nervous system.

KNEADING
Kneading is ideal for unlocking aching or tense

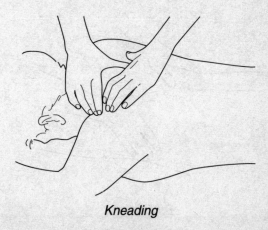

Kneading

muscles, in particular the trapezium muscle between the neck and shoulders. Both hands work together in a rhythmic sequence, alternately picking up and gently squeezing the tense muscle. The kneading gets deep enough to stimulate the lymph into removing the buildup of lactic acid.

FRICTION

Friction strokes are used to penetrate into deep muscle tissue. The heel of the hand, or the tips of the fingers, or the thumb may be used in a

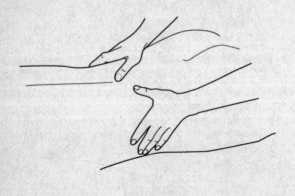

Friction

linear or circular motion. Thumb pressure is particularly effective for breaking down knotted muscle.

Neck and shoulder massage
What follows is a simple sequence that can be used to relieve headaches, loosen the shoulder muscles and provide a general feeling of relaxation.

Neck and shoulders – A
Stand behind your seated partner. Begin with

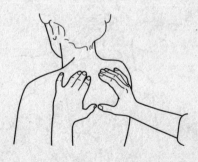

Neck and shoulders – A

effleurage, applying firm pressure with both hands. Start at the bottom of the shoulder blades up each side of the spine to the base of the neck. Move your hands apart across the top of the shoulders and then bring them gently down to the starting position. Repeat several times, finishing with a light return stroke.

NECK AND SHOULDERS – B
Stand at right angles to the side of your partner.

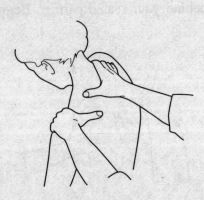

Neck and shoulders – B

Locate tension spots in the shoulders using your thumbs and then work these areas with the thumbs. The pressure can approach your partner's pain threshold but not exceed it.

NECK AND SHOULDERS – C
Place your left hand in an 'L' shape on your partner's shoulder. Applying firm pressure,

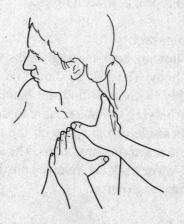

Neck and shoulders – C

move it slowly up the whole length of the shoulder. Repeat with your other hand. Continue repeating the sequence using alternate hands. Place one hand at the base of the back of the neck and move it gently up to the hairline, gently squeezing all the time. Return with a gentle stroke. Repeat several times. Without removing your hands, walk round to the other shoulder and repeat B and C. Move behind your partner and repeat A several times.

Back massage

The following back massage helps to relax the whole body. The strokes should be carried out smoothly, without lifting the hands from the back. Applying thumb pressure to the channels on either side of the spine on the upper back will help respiratory problems. The same stroke on the lower back can relieve constipation and menstrual discomfort.

BACK – A

Place your hands, facing each other, on either side

of the base of the spine. Move them up the back, using your body weight to apply pressure. Take your hands round the shoulders and return lightly down the sides of the body. Repeat several times before stopping to knead the shoulders. Work on one shoulder and then the other. Repeat the movement.

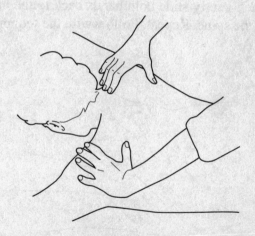

Back – A

BACK – B

Place your hands at waist level, with your thumbs in the hollows on either side of the spine and your fingers open and relaxed. Push your thumbs firmly up the channels for about two inches (six centimetres), relax them, and then move them back about one inch (two centimetres). Continue in this way up to the neck. Then gently slide both hands back to the base of the spine. Repeat. Follow with the sequence in A.

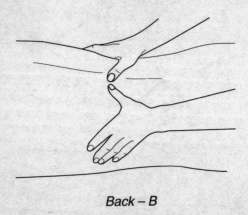

Back – B

Back – C

Place your hand flat across one side of your partner's back at the base of the spine. Apply firm palm pressure and work up to the shoulders. Follow closely with your other hand. Repeat using alternate hands. Work through the same sequence on the other side of the back, then repeat on both side several times. Finish by working through A.

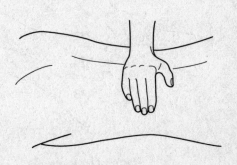

Back – C

BACK – D

Place your hands, facing up the back, on either side of the spine. Applying firm palm pressure, work from the base of the spine to chest level. Turn your fingers outwards and move your hands apart to the sides of the body. Repeat this stroke at waist and hip levels. Repeat the first movement in A several times.

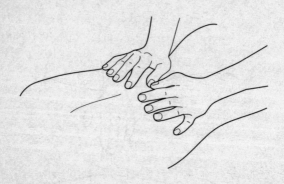

Back – D

Leg, feet and arm massage

LIMBS – A

Begin at the ankle and stroke vertically up the leg with one hand. Follow the same path with your other hand. Continue this sequence, using alternate hands.

Limbs – A

LIMBS – B

Raise your partner's foot and hold it with the knee at a right angle. Using the palm of your free hand, stroke firmly down the back of the leg from ankle to knee level. Use a light stroke

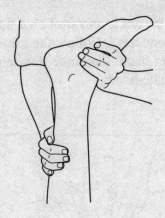

Limbs – B

to return to the ankle. Repeat the whole movement several times. If including the foot, work
through D and E next before repeating the full
sequence (A to B) on the other leg.

LIMBS – C
Help your partner to turn over, and begin by strok-

130

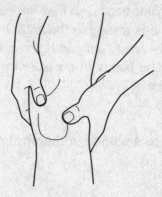

Limbs – C

ing with alternate hands up the whole leg, as in A. Then put your hands on either side of the knee and, using your thumbs to apply pressure, circle around the knee cap. If including the foot, bring your hands down to the ankle and use the sandwich stroke (D) on the front of the foot. Work through the full movement on the other leg.

LIMBS – D

With your partner lying face down, take one foot between your hands, so that the palm of your upper hand is resting in the arch. Press firmly, and slowly draw your hands down to the tip of the foot. Use plenty of pressure for this 'sandwich' stoke.

LIMBS – E

Hold the foot with your thumbs lying side by

Limbs – D

side behind the toes. Pull both thumbs back to the sides of the foot, then push them forward. Repeat this zig-zag movement as you work down to the heel. Then push firmly all the way back to the toes, keeping your thumbs side by side. Repeat the whole movement several times. Work through the whole sequence (D to E) on the other foot.

Limbs – E

LIMBS – F

Take hold of your partner's hand as in a firm handshake, and lift the arm up slightly, as far as the elbow. Gently place the palm of your fee hand across the top of the wrist and close your fingers round the raised arm. Apply firm pressure and slide your hand up to the elbow, or as far as the shoulder. Move your palm underneath the arm and use a light stroke to return to the wrist. Repeat several times.

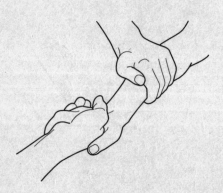

Limbs – F

LIMBS – G

Place your thumbs across the inside of your partner's wrist. Applying pressure with both your thumbs, make wide circles around the wrist area. Repeat F. As you finish, relax your hold on the wrist and pull off firmly and slowly in a sandwich stroke, as in D. Repeat the full sequence (F to G) on the other arm, finishing with the hand variation of D.

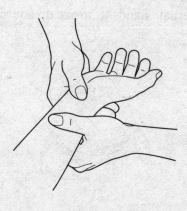

Limbs – G

Face and head massage
The following sequence encourages deep re-laxation. Gentle stroking of the forehead (B) can help to relieve stress-related tension and headaches, while pressure applied to the sides of the nose and along the cheekbones (C) alleviates nasal congestion and sinus problems. Scalp massage (D) stimulates cir-culation.

FACE AND HEAD – **A**
Use alternate hands to stroke up one side of the

Face and head – A

face, starting beneath the chin and working up towards the forehead. Work through the same movement on the other side of the face. Repeat several times. Finish by placing one palm across your partner's forehead, ready for the next stroke.

FACE AND HEAD – B

Begin by stroking up the forehead with alternate palms. Then place the pads of the middle three fingers of both hands in the centre of the forehead between the eyes. Draw them gently

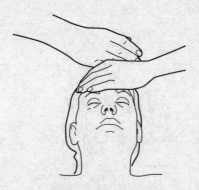

Face and head – B

apart across the brow and round the outside corner of the eyes. Lift off the middle two fingers and use your fourth fingers only to return under the eyes towards the nose.

FACE AND HEAD – C

Position your thumbs on your partner's forehead. Using the three middle fingers of both hands, press firmly against the sides of the nose. Continue along the top of the cheekbone, until you reach the temple. Keeping your thumbs in

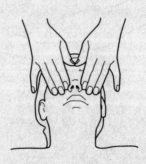

Face and head – C

position, return to the nose, pressing along the middle of the cheekbone.

FACE AND HEAD – D

Spread out the fingers and thumbs of both hands and place them on your partner's scalp. Keep them in position and begin to move the scalp muscle over the bone by applying gentle pressure and circling slowly and firmly on the spot. Stop occasionally to move to a different area, then begin again, working gradually over the whole scalp.

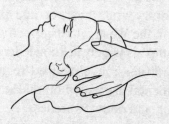

Face and head – D

Yoga

Yoga is a technique of self-awareness that has been practised in the East as a physical, psychological and philosophical discipline for over 5,000 years. The word 'yoga' derives from the Sanskrit *yuk*, meaning 'to bind together', and the aim of yoga is to integrate the mind and the body and commune with the universal process of being.

Yoga is not a religion and does not require adherence to any particular dogma; it is basically a technique for personal development, enabling people to explore and fulfil their physical and spiritual needs. Over the last quarter of the twentieth century yoga has become increasingly popular in the West, and its effectiveness in relieving stress is widely acknowledged within the medical profession. Practised regularly, yoga creates mental clarity, emotional stability, deep relaxation and body awareness.

One of the most popular forms of yoga, Hatha yoga, teaches techniques of physical control of the body through physical postures, known as *asanas,* and breathing techniques, called *pranayama.* The asanas make the body supple and benefit the neuromuscular system, each posture combining mental acuity with breathing techniques and a specific body movement.

The pranayama relax the body and calm the mind, increase circulation and stimulate the blood supply to all parts of the body. Breathing should be done through the nose, and it is important never to hold a breath. A movement is carried out during an exhalation, with a deep inhalation immediately before it.

Following a basic sequence of asanas is an excellent way to create the foundation of health and mental clarity. Focusing on certain positions can help with particular problems, but it is important to follow a structured sequence of asanas. You cannot extract a few and hope that they will be beneficial on their own. They must work together as the tension in one pose is complemented by the counter-stretch in another.

To use yoga at its real potential, it is important to practise at least three times a week. Any less than that and you are not giving the system a chance to affect or heal your body. It is also vital to stick to the relaxation sessions that begin and end each yoga session. Yoga is an excellent way of fighting tension, and buoying us up mentally and physically; these relaxation sessions are a vital component of each yoga session, and are designed to complement the main asanas.

The following sequence of asanas will give you some idea of the movements involved. But it is vital to learn the proper movements and breathing patterns from a trained yoga teacher.

Before you begin:
- Establish a convenient and regular time to practise.
- It is important not to have a full stomach.
- Wear comfortable and loose clothing.
- Use a clean, soft blanket or mat, thick enough to protect your spine and fit the length of your body.

- Perform each exercise slowly, carefully and mindfully. Force and strain must be avoided.

Yoga positions
CAT
Kneel on all fours with your hands shoulder-distance apart and your knees the same distance apart as your hands. Your elbows should remain straight throughout the entire exercise. Exhale while arching your back up high. Keep your head between your arms, looking at your abdomen. Hold this pose for a few seconds. Inhale,

The cat helps to strengthen the spine, improve posture and revitalise the whole body.

as you slowly hollow your back to a concave position. Raise your head and look up. Hold again. Repeat the sequence five to ten times, creating a slow flowing movement of the two postures. Relax.

TREE

Stand with both feet together, arms loosely by your side. Focus your eyes on an imaginary spot directly ahead of you. Bring the right foot up and place the sole against the inside of the left

The tree promotes concentration, balance and stability of body and mind

high as possible. When balanced, raise both arms simultaneously, placing the palms together over your head. Hold for 30 seconds. Gently lower your arms. Release your foot from your thigh. Repeat the sequence with the other foot. Relax.

TRIANGLE

Stand with your feet about three feet (less than a metre) apart. Inhale and raise your arms sideways

The triangle helps to calm the nerves, acts to remove toxins from the body, and promotes good health in general.

to shoulder level. Turn your left foot ninety degrees to the left and your right foot forty-five degrees to the left. Exhale and bend from the waist to touch the left foot with the left hand. The right arm points up, forming a straight line with the left arm. Turn your face towards the upraised hand. Hold for ten seconds. Inhale and return to a standing position. Turn your feet to the right in the same manner and perform the exercise on the right side – slowly, smoothly and carefully. Relax.

SIMPLE TWIST

Sit with outstretched legs. Pull the right leg towards the body. Place the right foot across the left leg on the floor, next to the left knee. Inhale. Twist the upper body to the right, placing both hands on the right side of the body on the floor. Look over the right shoulder and exhale. Hold for at least ten seconds. Inhale as you slowly move out of the posture and repeat on the other side. This is a gentle posture that is easy to perform. Relax.

The simple twist helps to strengthen the spine, improve posture and promote psychological balance and self-confidence.

COBRA

Lie face down. Place the palms on the floor under the shoulders, fingers turned slightly inwards. Slowly lift the forehead, the nose, the chin, and the entire upper body, up to the navel. The weight rests on both hands, the pelvis, and the legs. Keep the elbows slightly bent, and do not allow the shoulders to hunch up towards the ears. Hold for ten seconds, focusing your attention on the lower back. Very slowly lower your

The cobra increases blood supply to the abdominal organs and helps to relieve digestive problems and correct kidney malfunctions.

trunk to the floor, then the chin, the nose, and the forehead. Relax.

PLOUGH
Lie on your back, arms by your sides, palms down. Slowly raise your legs and trunk off the floor. Supporting your hips with both hands, bring your legs slightly over your head. Keep

*The plough helps to reinvigorate the entire nervous
system, removing fatigue, listlessness and exhaustion.
It is of particular benefit to the pancreas and endocrine
glands.*

your legs as straight as possible. Supporting your
back with both hands, continue lifting your legs
up and over your head until the toes come to
rest on the floor behind your head. Only when
you are quite comfortable in the position, release the hold on your back and place your arms
flat on the floor. Hold only for ten seconds in
the beginning. After your body becomes accus-

tomed to this position, you may hold it longer. Very slowly unroll your body to the starting position. Relax.

FORWARD BEND

Make sure you are well warmed up before attempting this posture. Sit with your legs stretched out in front of you, knees very straight. Inhale and stretch your arms above your head. Exhale and very

The forward bend slows the respiratory rate to produce a calm and relaxed state of mind. It also increases the suppleness of the spine and improves blood circulation – which helps to regenerate the abdominal organs and improve digestion.

slowly and smoothly bend forward from the hips (*not from the waist*) to grasp your toes. If at first this seems difficult, clasp instead your ankles,

150

calves, or knees. It is important that your legs remain straight. Continue to bend forward and down, aiming to touch your knees with your head. Hold for at least ten seconds and observe your breath. Release your hold and very slowly unroll your spine, returning to a sitting position. Repeat twice.

SALUTE TO THE SUN

This classic exercise coordinates breathing with variations of six yoga poses in a flowing rhythmic way that stretches and relaxes your body and your mind.

Start by facing east, standing up as straight as you can without forcing it, with your feet together. Inhale and visualise the sun just beginning to rise. Exhale and bring the palms of the hands on to your chest as if you were praying.

Inhale again, stretching your arms overhead as you do so, pushing the pelvis forward a little, and look up at your hands.

Breathe out, bending slowly from your waist until, ideally, your hands are touching the floor in front of or beside your feet. (Don't force this: if you can't reach the floor, let your hands hold on to the lowest part of your legs they can reach.)

Breathe in and lunge forward by bending your left knee to a right angle and stepping your right foot back. Turn your toes right under and straighten your body from head to heel.

Holding your breath, move the left foot back, toes curled, until you are in the classic push-up position.

Now exhale and drop your knees to the floor, with your bottom up. Bend the elbows and bring your chest and chin to the floor. Continue breathing out and lower the whole body to the floor, straightening your legs and keeping your toes curled under.

Inhale, pushing down on your hands and slowly lifting your head as you straighten the elbows. Arch your back upwards like a snake before it strikes.

Breathe out and, with the buttocks as high in the air as you can raise them and the head down, form a pyramid.

Breathe in and lunge forward by bending your right knee and stepping your right foot forward between your hands.

When you breathe out, straighten your right leg and bring the left foot next to the right. Lift your buttocks high until you are touching your toes.

Inhale and slowly lift the spine, visualising it unroll one vertebra at a time. Raise your head and look up, bringing your arms straight overhead, and bring the image of the rising sun back to mind.

Breathe out and slowly bring your arms back to the sides, allowing the sun to glow brighter and brighter in your mind's eye.

Salute the sun six times at first, gradually increasing the number of repetitions until you are comfortably doing the routine 24 times.

Traditional Chinese medicine

About 2,500 years ago, deep in the mountains of Northern China, Taoist priests practised Qi Gong – meditative movement revealing and cultivating the vital life force. They believed this force, Qi (pronounced 'chi' in China, 'ki' in Japan), was inseparable from life itself. They discovered that Qi animated not only body and earth, but was the energetic force of the entire universe. Traditional Chinese medicine is a philosophy of preserving health, and is based first and foremost on an understanding of the ultimate power of Qi. In contrast to much of Western medicine, traditional Chinese medicine is a preventative practice, strengthening the immune system to ward off disease.

In traditional Chinese medicine, Qi is manifested both as *yin* (cold, dark, and 'interior'), and *yang* (warm, light, and 'exterior'). In fact, Qi is present in all the opposites we experience, such as night and day, hot and cold, growth and decay. And although yin and yang may be perceived as opposites, they are actually inseparable. The recognition of one is essential to the recognition of the other. The balance between them is like the motion of night and day; at the instant darkness reaches its zenith at midnight, the cycle has begun to flow steadily towards dawn. At noon, the zenith of light, the day begins slowly to turn towards the darkness of night. All the internal organs of the body are subject to this nocturnal–diurnal swing of the universe.

This world view further holds that Qi, manifesting as yin/yang, makes up the universe in the form of five elements: wood, fire, earth, metal, and water. These five elements also represent our bodily constitution as human beings, making us one with the universe. Qi flows into our bodies, up from the earth in its yin form and down from the heavens in its yang form. The energy channels in our bodies through which it moves are called 'meridians'.

These meridians do not directly correspond to any anatomical component recognised by Western medicine. The best way to understand the flow of Qi through the meridians is to compare it to the flow of blood in our veins and arteries. If our blood does not reach our toes, they become dead. If our blood does not flow freely, we have high or low blood pressure. If our blood clots, we have an embolism or a stroke. Similarly, unbalanced or stagnant Qi can cause many diseases and ailments. In fact, traditional Chinese medicine is based on the principle that every illness, ailment, and discomfort in the body can be explained in terms of an imbalance of Qi.

Each meridian is related to one of the five elements. For example, the heart meridian is related to the element fire, the kidney and bladder to water. Along the meridians are pressure points, or 'gateways', special places where Qi can become blocked. With the help of a trained practitioner, its flow can be freed and balance restored.

Out of the belief system of traditional Chinese medicine arose many healing methods, all directed to the balancing of Qi. These include acupuncture, shiatsu, Tai Chi Ch'uan and herbalism.

Acupuncture

This is a form of traditional Chinese medicine that uses the gentle insertion of hair-fine needles into specific points on the body to stimulate the flow of one's Qi, or natural healing en-

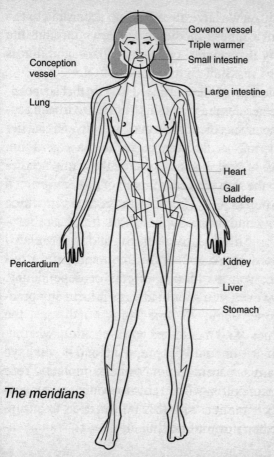

- Govenor vessel
- Triple warmer
- Small intestine
- Conception vessel
- Large intestine
- Lung
- Heart
- Gall bladder
- Pericardium
- Kidney
- Liver
- Stomach

The meridians

ergy. As we have already seen, according to ancient Chinese medicine Qi flows through the body in channels, called meridians, and illness is the result of an imbalance of Qi.

Most people are surprised to learn that acupuncture needles are very thin (from ten to fifteen acupuncture needles can fit into one conventional hypodermic needle). Acupuncturists can attain a high level of skill in gently placing these tiny needles into the skin with a minimum of discomfort.

Acupuncture excels in those areas in which conventional medicine offers limited relief – chronic disease, pain control, and stress-related disorders. Acupuncture treatments are drug-free; you avoid side effects or dependency. However, you should always inform any practitioner about all preexisting conditions, the names of all medicines you are taking, whether you are, or could be, pregnant, and if you have a cardiac pacemaker or cosmetic implants. Your acupuncturist will be able to evaluate your specific situation with this information to ensure the best form of treatment.

Shiatsu

Shiatsu is a Japanese healing art combining the principles of traditional Chinese medicine with practices similar to those of acupuncture but performed without needles. Shiatsu is a balance – a dance – between practitioner and receiver, in which the healing power of both build upon each other to clear and balance the vital life force known as Qi.

Shiatsu is a Japanese word: *shi* meaning 'finger', and *atsu* meaning 'pressure'. But shiatsu is more than acupressure. It is a combination of many different techniques, including pressing, hooking, sweeping, shaking, rotating, grasping, vibrating, patting, plucking, lifting, pinching, rolling, brushing, and, in one variation – barefoot shiatsu – it includes walking on the person's back, legs, and feet.

But these are merely the physical techniques. With an awareness of psychological and spiritual implications, shiatsu has become, indeed, a kind of dance between giver and receiver. A unique rapport develops between the practitioner

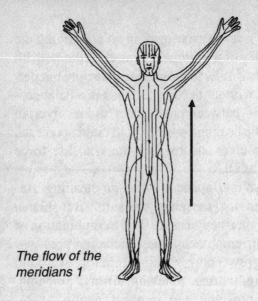

*The flow of the
meridians 1*

and client, because shiatsu relies on the simple but powerful experience of touch to awaken the client's own self-healing powers. This 'touch communication' between practitioner and client is fundamental to all healing methods.

No needles, creams, machines, devices, or other paraphernalia are needed for the experience of a

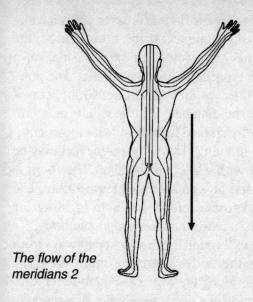

*The flow of the
meridians 2*

complete shiatsu session. The practitioner uses
gentleness, fluidity, and rhythmical motion to work
with the imbalances in the client's Qi. Progressively, over a number of sessions, the client can
learn how to assist in the balance of his or her own
Qi.

Some shiatsu practitioners use a massage table; others use the floor in order to apply a wider variety of techniques. If the floor is used, the person lies on a futon, an exercise mat, or a mattress especially made for shiatsu. The practitioner then works by kneeling, sitting, crawling, and standing near the client. The client remains fully clothed for shiatsu with loose, comfortable clothing. The body and/or feet may be covered with a sheet or blanket. The room is maintained at a comfortable temperature, and soft background music can help to bring the person to a relaxed state of mind and body.

Qi flows through the meridian pathways in all parts of the body. There are more than 300 acupoints along the way. Acupuncture requires the insertion of a single needle for each acupoint selected. In shiatsu the application to these meridian pathways by the practitioner's fingers, hands, knees, or elbows covers several of these critical points simultaneously.

Continual diagnosis is part of the treatment. It is a supportive system: reciprocal, interdependent, and cooperative between giver and receiver.

The healing energy and awareness build in this synergy for both practitioner and client. Throughout this duet in movement, the use of the practitioner's two hands – mother hand and messenger hand – allows continuous motion. The client experiences no pain, but rather a comfortable feeling of partnership in the awakening of powerful self-healing forces. Mutual meditation on the origin of deep breathing clears the mind, allowing fresh oxygen to replenish and rejuvenate the internal organs, so that a deeper sense of self-awareness evolves and healing occurs.

In the practice of shiatsu, each person is primarily responsible for his or her own health and wellbeing. This contrasts with the Western belief that the medical practitioner is principally responsible for our health. In Western medicine an awareness of the unique significance of touch – the essential form of communication between two human beings in the fight to subdue pain – has almost disappeared; certainly it has become minimal. Ironically, in all times and all cultures, the importance of touch – just touch itself – has been acknowledged as a primary means to mitigate pain. In the hurried rounds of the Western hospital doctors checking hospital charts, this important fact is largely ignored.

Simple Shiatsu procedures

Sit quietly on the floor, on a cushion. Place one hand on top of the other, over the navel. Clear your mind and concentrate on deep breathing, focusing on a starting point one-and-a-half inches (four centimetres) below the navel. This point is known as 'ki-kai' or 'ocean of energy'. Breathe deeply, and perhaps (to be sure your mind is clear of its daily clutter) you might hum softly as you slowly breathe out. These sounds have a soothing effect.

After a few minutes of deep breathing, lean forward onto your hands as you exhale your humming vibrations. Now inhale slowly as you gently straighten the spine and return to your original sitting position.

Repeat five times.

Now clasp both hands so that they interlock in the Vs between the index finger and thumb. You are touching a major acupoint, large intestine number 4, called 'go kuku' ('meeting mountains'). Press the thumb, leaning in towards the base of the index finger. Hold the pressure for five seconds, release for five seconds. Repeat for relief from headache, toothache, menstrual cramps, or gastritis.

This simple form of self-shiatsu affects the internal organs. You can increase a specific effect through your focus. For example, when you are bending forward, concentrate on the kidneys in the lumbar area – your lower back. This will strengthen your Qi.

Alexander Technique

The Alexander Technique is a practical and simple method of learning to focus attention on how we use ourselves during daily activities. F. M. Alexander (1869–1955), an Australian therapist, demonstrated that the difficulties many people experience in learning, in control of perform-

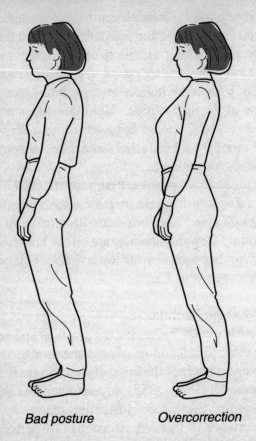

Bad posture   *Overcorrection*

Correct posture

ance, and in physical functioning are caused by unconscious habits. These habits interfere with your natural poise and your capacity to learn. When you stop interfering with the innate coordination of the body, you can take on more complex activities with greater self-confidence and presence of mind. It is about learning to bring into our conscious awareness the choices we make, as we make them. Gentle hands-on and verbal instruction reveal the underlying principles of human coordination, allow the student to experience and observe their own habitual patterns, and give the means for release and change.

Most of us are unconsciously armouring ourselves in relation to our environment. This is hard work and often leaves us feeling anxious, alienated, depressed, draggy, and unlovable. Armouring is a deeply unconscious behaviour that has probably gone on since early childhood, maybe even since infancy. Yet it is a habit we can unlearn in the present through careful self-observation. We can unlearn our use of excess tension in our thoughts, movements, and relationships.

An Alexander teacher guides a person, as he or she moves, to use less tension. The instructor works by monitoring the student's posture and reminding him or her to implement tiny changes in movement to eradicate the habit of excess tension. Students learn to stop bracing themselves up, or to stop collapsing into themselves. As awareness grows, it becomes easier to recognise and relinquish the habit of armouring and dissolve the artificial barriers we put between ourselves and others.

An analogy of this process can be seen in the now familiar three-dimensional Magic Eye Art.

With our ordinary way of looking we see only a mass of dots. When we shift to the 'Magic Eye' way of seeing, a three-dimensional object appears. Through the Alexander Technique a similar type of experience is available. But the three-dimensional object we experience is ourselves.

Although the Alexander Technique does not treat specific symptoms, you can encourage a marked improvement in overall health, alertness, and performance by consciously eliminating harmful habits that cause physical and emotional stress, and by becoming more aware of how you engage in your activities.

Aromatherapy

In the past the human sense of smell was crucial to our survival – we could smell intruders, sense which plants were poisonous and track game through their odour. Obviously, the need for this ability has lessened, and we are now more likely to appreciate the smell of the latest perfumery sensation, or suffer under the stench of cigarettes or cigars. However, we are still extremely susceptible to smell – both personal and environmental. We all have our own unique smell (pherones), apart from body odour, and while our recognition may be subconscious, it has more effect on our responses and behaviour than we may realise. Our emotions and physical harmony can be effected through our sense of smell. The effect of pleasant or unpleasant smells on the harmony of our bodies is well documented, and utilised through the art of aromatherapy.

Aromatherapy uses essential oils, which are extracted from aromatic plants and trees. A holistic medicine, it shares the same principles as acupuncture, reflexology and herbal medicine, to name a few. These arts are complementary and work on the principle of promoting mental serenity and bodily health – treating the person as one entity.

The therapy works from the principle that life itself is utterly intangible, that its core or essence cannot be seen, felt or analysed. When we talk about life, we talk about our souls and emotions, as well as our physical and physiological presence. The Chinese call it Qi, and it represents the energy that propels us through each day of our lives and creates the world around us. This force is present in every plant and tree, and aromatherapy deals with extracting this organic 'essence' and using it to enhance, cure and protect. Essential oils can affect mood, alleviate fatigue, reduce anxiety and promote relaxation. When inhaled they work on the nervous system and brain through stimulation of the olfactory nerves. When absorbed through the skin, stronger components are released into the bloodstream.

The origin of aromatherapy is hard to pinpoint. Records show that the Egyptians were the first civilisation truly to investigate and implement organic essences for cosmetic, embalming and holistic use. For instance, they used red ochre to colour lips and cheeks and *kohl* (an early eyeliner) to define eyes. Their priests were the first to dictate the use of essences and oils, but as in most civilisations, popular use ensured that their benefits, both cosmetic and medical, soon impregnated all aspects of their society.

The art eventually reached Britain through trade with the Greeks and the Romans; the earliest written British record appeared in the thirteenth century. Interest waned in the nineteenth century because of the development of chemical copies of plant oils. But the twentieth century's renewed interest in the natural treatments and therapies has pushed oil extraction and implementation techniques to the forefront of the holistic industry. Pure essential oils are now used in toiletries, foods and medicines, and their properties are scientifically recognised.

The raw materials of aromatherapy are essential oils – the personalities of the plants, fruits and herbs. Scientifically this essence is called the hormone or blood supply of the plant. In reality they are the volatile (evaporating readily in air) and odorous liquid elements of aromatic plants. Their chemistry is complex, but usually includes alcohols, esters, ketones, aldehydes and terpenes. These oils are present in tiny droplets in roots, flowers, barks, rinds and resins – all in varying quantities. For example, up to 100 kilos of rose petals produces 1–2 litres of oil, but 100 kilos of lavender plants yield around 3 litres of oil. The oils are very kinetic by nature and constantly changing in chemical composition, from day to day and season to season. Soil and weather also have a huge effect on their make-up, so they have to be picked with scientific precision.

There are many methods to extract oils, such as hand expression, enfleurage and maceration, but the most modern and most commonly used method is steam distillation. Making use of the volatile nature of the oils and the fact that they are insoluble in water, this method also impregnates the steam with the fragrant essence of the water, thus creating useful by-products. Orange and rose water are two popular examples. Because of their fragile nature, oils must be kept in bottles, in cool dark place to protect their properties.

Essential oils are adaptable. They can added

to a bath, with the steam releasing their perfume; they can be inhaled directly from a bottle; or they can be incorporated into massage oil. This can have a dual effect: the oils can be absorbed into the skin, and the massage has additional beneficial effect.

You can find oils that solve a range of disorders. Basil, bergamot, camomile, clary, jasmine, juniper, neroli, orange blossom, rose, rosemary, sage, ylang ylang are used in treatments of faulty circulation, fluid retention, lethargy and depression. Sandalwood, sage, cypress, marjoram and rose are good for nervous tension, sleeplessness and irritability. In dealing with catarrh and sinus problems, cedarwood, frankincense, hyssop and eucalyptus are effective.

Oils for stress management
BASIL
Basil helps to invigorate the body and spirit; refreshes the mind to improve concentration; and is especially effective when tired. It is an excel-

lent nerve tonic after a stressful day. It has a sweet liquorice-like fragrance, and blends well with lavender, bergamot, clary sage and geranium.

BENZOIN TINCTURE
A warm, soothing, comforting oil. Add to carrier oil or cream for protecting skin against chapping or cracking.

BERGAMOT
The lovely light citrus aroma of this oil relaxes and refreshes. Use in a vaporiser to disperse unpleasant odours. Add one drop to cooled boiled water as a mouthwash. It also blends well with other oils.

Warning: Do not use this on the skin before going out into strong sunlight or using a sunbed: it can increase susceptibility to sunburn.

BLACK PEPPER
One of the oldest known spices, the oil's pungent aroma has a stimulating and warming ef-

fect. It blends well with rosemary, marjoram and lavender, but should only be used in small amounts.

Warning: Black pepper can be a skin irritant, so must be used with care.

Cajeput
Improves mood and increases resistance to infections. A good 'unwinding' oil, it can be used in a steam inhalation to help clear the nasal passages, and is also useful in treating oily skin and spots.

Warning: Cajeput is a stimulant and an irritant and must be used with care.

Camomile Roman
This oil is well known for its strong, soothing effect on the mind and body. It can be used to calm nerves, soothe headaches, relieve insomnia, and alleviate menstrual disorders. It is also one of the few essential oils that can be used on inflamed skin conditions.

Camomile

CAMPHOR

This oil can be used to help alleviate cold symptoms and is also useful for treating oily or spotty skin.

Warning: Camphor should be used sparingly and completely avoided by those suffering from epilepsy.

CARDAMOM SEED

The sweet, spicy, warming fragrance of cardamom has been enjoyed since the days of the ancient Egyptians, who used it as a perfume and incense. It can be used as an aid to digestion and makes a refreshing bath oil.

CEDARWOOD
Recognised as a therapeutic oil from ancient times, cedarwood has a soothing and steadying effect. The oil is also useful for protecting oily and blemished skin, and as an inhalant it helps to relieve coughs and colds.

Warning: Do not use cedarwood during pregnancy.

CINNAMON
A warming and stimulating oil that is traditionally used to alleviate digestive disorders. It also has antiseptic properties and has a cleansing effect.

Warning: Cinnamon is a powerful irritant and must not be used on the skin.

CLARY SAGE
Noted for its soothing, relaxing and warming effect, it contains a hormone-like compound similar to oestrogen that regulates hormonal

balance. Massage on the muscles and abdomen for relief of menstrual discomfort.

Warning: Do not use during pregnancy.

CLOVE

An antiseptic oil used to relieve toothache.

Warning: Clove is a powerful skin irritant and should be used carefully. Do not use during pregnancy.

CORIANDER

A sweet-smelling, spicy essence, it makes a good massage blend to relieve stiffness and muscle ache. In the bath it is refreshing and stimulating.

CYPRESS

With its smoky woody fragrance, it refreshes, restores and tones. It is an astringent oil useful for refreshing and caring for oily and blemished skin. As a natural deodorant, it can also be used as an antiperspirant and is good for sweaty feet. Blends well with lavender and sandalwood.

EUCALYPTUS

This is a powerful antiseptic widely used to alleviate the symptoms of colds and flu. Use as a chest rub and in a vaporiser to keep the air germ-free. Blends well with lavender and pine.

FENNEL

Fennel has a sweet aniseed-like aroma, which makes it pleasant for skin care. As a massage

Fennel

oil it is good for the digestive system, and can promote breast firming and milk production, but use sparingly.

Warning: Fennel can be a skin irritant. Do not use it on young children. Do not use if pregnant. Do not use if suffering from epilepsy.

FRANKINCENSE

This oil soothes, warms and aids meditation. It has been used for centuries, and burnt on alters and in temples. It has a comforting effect, and by slowing down breathing and controlling tension it helps to focus the mind. It is excellent for toning and caring for mature or aging skin (it is supposed to have rejuvenating qualities – the Egyptians used it in rejuvenation face-masks).

GERANIUM

A balancing oil for the mind and body. Fresh, floral and sweet-smelling, it relaxes, restores and maintains stability of the emotions. It is useful in massage for treating eczema and psoriasis. It blends well with other floral oils, and, mixed with lavender and bergamot, produces a delightful room freshener.

GINGER
A warm and penetrating oil that is good for nausea and sickness. Blend with orange for warming winter baths. It blends especially well with orange and other citrus oils. Use in small amounts.

GRAPEFRUIT
This essence refreshes and uplifts the spirit. It has a lovely fresh aroma that can help with nervous exhaustion.

Warning: Do not use grapefruit on the skin in direct sunlight.

HYSSOP
This fragrance was sacred to the Greeks and the Hebrews, who used hyssop brooms to clean out sacred places. It has a warm and vibrant aroma that can be used to promote

alertness and clarity of thought. When used in a fragrance it can help to protect rooms from infection. It is also useful for treating colds and flu.

Warning: This powerful oil should not to be used when pregnant or suffering from epilepsy or high blood pressure.

JASMINE

This oil is emotionally warming. It also relaxes, soothes, uplifts and helps self-confidence. It is good for stress and general anxiety. It only needs to be used in very small quantities. It is very expensive because large numbers of blossoms must be gathered at night, when their scent is at its highest, to produce only a few drops of oil.

JUNIPER

Its fresh woody aroma tones and stimulates. It has a cleansing effect on the body and a calming effect on the emotions. It is reputed to strengthen the immune system.

Juniper

Warning: Juniper should not be used when pregnant.

LAVENDER

This is undoubtedly the most versatile and useful oil. No home should be without it. It relaxes, soothes, restores and balances your body and mind. Excellent for refreshing tired muscles, feet and head. Add a drop to the pillow or sheet for a restful night. Blends happily with most other oils.

LEMON

An astringent and antiseptic oil that cleanses, refreshes, cools and stimulates. Useful for oily skin, it can be used to lighten dull, stained hands or to tone and condition nails and cuticles. It blends well with other oils. *Warning*: Do not use lemon on the skin in direct sunlight. Dilute to 1 per cent and use only three drops in a bath as it may cause skin irritation.

LEMONGRASS

An antiseptic and astringent oil that has a refreshing, cleansing and stimulating effect on the mind and body. Its sweet, powerful 'lemony' aroma makes it a good choice as a refreshing and deodorising room fragrance.

Warning: Dilute to 1 per cent and use only three drops in a bath as it may cause skin irritation.

MARJORAM

Popular with the ancient Greeks, it soothes, comforts and warms. Useful on tired muscles and for massage. It can also be used to regulate the nervous system and treat insomnia. It is pleasant in a hot bath, especially blended with lavender.

Warning: Do not use during pregnancy. It has a sedative effect, so use carefully.

MELISSA

A popular garden herb known also as 'lemon balm', this has a soothing, but uplifting, effect on the mind and body.

Warning: Do not use melissa on the skin in direct sunlight. Dilute to 1 per cent and use only three drops in a bath as it may cause skin irritation.

MYRRH

This is a smoky, mysterious oil. Add to a cream for protecting skin against cracking and chapping in the cold. Add to gargle and mouthwash.

Warning: Do not use myrrh during pregnancy.

NEROLI
This is the most effective oil for alleviating the symptoms of stress. Its exquisite aroma soothes, relaxes, uplifts the spirit and helps maintain confidence. It can be used to improve sluggish circulation, and to relieve tension and anxiety.

ORANGE
A warm, comforting oil that soothes, restores and uplifts the spirit. Blend with spicy oils for cheering baths. Use as a massage oil for the digestive system. It also encourages restful sleep.
   Warning: Do not use on the skin in direct sunlight. Dilute to 2 per cent and use only four or five drops in a bath as it may cause skin irritation.

PATCHOULI
A sweet, musky oil that soothes and uplifts the spirit. Useful in protecting dry, mature or blemished skin.

PEPPERMINT

One of the most important essential oils, it stimulates, refreshes, cools, restores and uplifts the mind and body. Add to a massage blend for the digestive system. It is excellent for refreshing tired head and feet. Sniff from the bottle or one drop on a handkerchief to revive energy during long journeys. Add a few drops to the car dashboard to help stay alert, stimulate clear thinking and remain fresh. Blended with rosemary and juniper, it makes an excellent morning bath.

Warning: Some aromatherapists warn against the use of peppermint when pregnant. Dilute to 1 per cent and use no more than three drops in the bath as it may cause irritation to sensitive skin.

PINE

Pine has a strong, fresh, resinous aroma and a powerful antiseptic and invigorating quality.

Warning: Dilute and use with care as pine oil may cause skin irritation.

ROSEMARY

A popular oil that has a variety of mental and physical benefits. It refreshes tired muscles, clears the mind, and aids concentration. It combats fatigue and clears a stuffy atmosphere.

Warning: Do not use rosemary if pregnant, have high blood pressure or suffer from epilepsy.

ROSE OTTO

Called the queen of flowers, the exquisite aroma is emotionally soothing and helps to maintain self-confidence. It is excellent for skincare; perfect for dry, mature, ageing or thread-veined skin.

Warning: Avoid during the first four months of pregnancy.

ROSEWOOD

This oil has a pleasant and flowery aroma that is relaxing and deodorising. Add to massage oil to help combat tired muscles – especially after vigorous exercise. It has a steadying and balancing affect on nerves, and is useful during exams. It is also a good antidepressant and may help to alleviate migraine

Sage

This oil has a calming effect on the central nervous system. It may also help with menstrual and digestive disorders.

Warning: Do not use sage when pregnant or suffering from epilepsy.

Sandalwood

This oil has a rich, woody, sweet aroma, and is traditionally burnt as an aid to meditation.

Tea tree

This oil has powerful antiseptic, antifungal and antiviral properties. It acts as a stimulant to the immune system and has a wide range of medicinal uses.

Warning: May cause irritation to sensitive skins.

THYME

This has been used for centuries as a medicinal and culinary herb. It has a strong pungent aroma and can be used as a vapour to alleviate nasal congestion.

Warning: Do not use when pregnant or if you have high blood pressure. Dilute to no more than 2 per cent before use. It may cause irritation to sensitive skins.

YLANG YLANG

The name means 'flower of flowers'. This sweet oil has a soothing and relaxing effect in times of tension and stress. It is also ideal for both oily and dry skins and can be used as a hair rinse (use two drops in water). It blends well with lemon and bergamot.

Autogenics

This is another relaxation technique derived from the principles of Eastern meditation. The participant learns to switch off the flight-or-fight response to stressful situations through progressive self-relaxation.

The system was originally devised by Johannes H. Schultz, a German psychiatrist and hypnotherapist. The technique is a combination of controlled breathing, hypnotherapy and positive thinking. Autogenics places heavy emphasis on self-belief and self-determination. Many studies of the system have confirmed that it is an excellent technique of deep relaxation, and can help to alleviate or control many stress-related disorders, such as phobias, anxiety, high blood pressure, migraines, insomnia and muscle tension. It also helps to improve concentration and overall coordination.

Many trained autogenics practitioners are also qualified psychotherapists or counsellors. They help to educate a person to control and reduce stress responses, to achieve deep relaxation, promote inner harmony, and restore emotional and physical wellbeing.

Biofeedback

This refers to the use of monitoring equipment to measure and control levels of relaxation. Training can be given after the scientific data is examined.

Although great feats of body and mind control have been reported in Eastern medicine for centuries, it has only been in the past two decades that Western medicine has accepted the fact that humans can, indeed, regulate their own heart rate, circulation, temperature, muscle tension, and other body functions that were mostly thought to operate only automatically. That acceptance came largely through the development of the biofeedback machine, which teaches people to become aware of various body functions and to control them with conscious intent, using relaxation and mental imagery techniques.

Today biofeedback is widely used for the treatment of chronic pain and stress-related disorders. Even astronauts have used biofeedback to control the nausea of space sickness.

If you go for biofeedback therapy, you will be asked to sit in a comfortable chair in front of a machine that looks like a TV set. Electrode sensors (wires) from the biofeedback machine will be taped to your body, usually on your forehead, neck, back, or forefinger. With the help of relaxing music or a taped voice that suggests relaxation techniques, you will be asked to reduce the muscle tension throughout your body. Later you way also be asked to slow your heart rate, even warm your hands by increasing their blood flow. While you're trying to accomplish these feats, the machine measures your muscle tension, heart rate and blood flow, and 'feeds back' how well you are doing. This feedback can be in the form of audible beeps, pictures, or graphic lines.

After learning what the correct response feels like by working with the machine and practising at home, you should eventually be able to achieve the same response without the machine.

Floatation

A form of sensory deprivation, floatation involves lying face up in an enclosed, dark tank of warm, heavily salted water. There is no sound, except perhaps some natural music to bring the client into a dreamlike state. It is exceptionally refreshing and induces a deep, relaxing sleep.

Herbalism

The use of medicinal herbs to alleviate illness is based on ancient techniques. When used properly, traditional herbs are non-addictive, have no side effects and can have impressive results. Herbs are particularly useful in treating nervous tension, depression, insomnia, PMS, nervous headaches and migraines. Herbal remedies are also extremely important in helping to reduce stress by their effects on the immune, circulatory and neuromuscular systems.

Herbalism is sometimes maligned as a collection of home-made remedies to be applied in a placebo fashion to one symptom or another, provided the ailment is not too serious and provided there is a powerful chemical wonder-drug at the ready to suppress any 'real' symptoms. We often forget, however, that botanical medicine provides a complete system of healing and disease prevention. It is the oldest and most natural form of medicine. Its record of efficacy and safety spans centuries and covers every country worldwide. Because herbal medicine is holistic medicine, it is, in fact, able to look beyond the symptoms to the underlying systemic imbalance; when skilfully applied by a trained practitioner, herbal medicine offers very real and permanent solutions to concrete problems, many of them seemingly intractable to pharmaceutical intervention.

Nowhere is the efficacy of herbalism more evident than in problems related to the nervous system. Stress, anxiety, tension and depression are intimately connected with most illness. Few health practitioners would argue with the influence of nervous anxiety in pathology. Nervous tension is generally acknowledged by doctors to contribute to duodenal and gastric ulceration, ulcerative colitis, irritable bowel syndrome and many other gut-related pathologies.

We know also, from physiology, that when a person is depressed, the secretion of hydrochloric acid – one of the main digestive juices – is also reduced so that digestion and absorption are rendered less efficient. Anxiety, on the other hand, can lead to the release of adrenaline and stimulate the overproduction of hydrochloric acid and result in a state of acidity that may exacerbate the pain of an inflamed ulcer. In fact, whenever the voluntary nervous system (our conscious anxiety) interferes with the autonomic processes (the automatic nervous regulation that in health is never made conscious), illness is the result.

Herbalists rely on their knowledge of botanical remedies to rectify this type of human malfunction. The medical herbalist will treat a stubborn dermatological problem using 'alternatives' specific to the skin problem, and then apply circulatory stimulants to aid in the removal of toxins from the area, with remedies to reinforce other organs of elimination, such as the liver and kidneys. Under such natural treatment, free of any discomforting side effects, the patient can feel confident and relaxed – perhaps for the first time in many months.

Curiously, this is an approach that has never been taken up by orthodox medicine. There, the usual treatment of skin problems involves suppression of symptoms with steroids. However, the use of conventional antihistamines or benzodiazepines often achieves less lasting benefit to the patient because of the additional burden of side effects, such as drowsiness, increased toxicity, and long-term drug dependence.

Herbs, on the other hand, are free from toxicity and habituation. Because they are organic substances and not man-made synthetic molecules, they possess an affinity for the human organism. They are extremely efficient in balancing the nervous system. Restoring a sense of wellbeing and relaxation is necessary for optimum health and for the process of self-healing.

Naturally, the choice of a treatment should be based upon a thorough health assessment and the experience and training of a qualified herbal practitioner. The herbalist will then prepare and prescribe herbal remedies in a variety of different forms, such as infusions, loose teas, suppositories, inhalants, lotions, tinctures, tablets and pills. Many of these preparations are available for home use from chemists, health shops and mail-order suppliers.

Herbs for stress management

CAMOMILE

This has a relaxing effect on the mind and body. It is an excellent sedative for anxiety and muscle tenseness. Many people enjoy its benefits in the form of camomile tea.

VALERIAN

This is the ideal tranquilliser. The rhizomes of this plant contain a volatile oil (which includes valerianic acid), volatile alkaloids (including chatinine), and iridoids (valepotriates), which

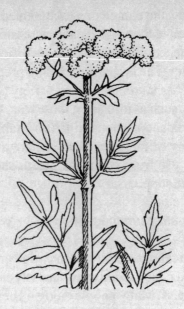

Valerian

have been shown to reduce anxiety and aggression. So effective is Valerian in relieving anxiety while maintaining normal mental awareness, that it enables us to continue the most complicated mental exercise without drowsiness, loss of consciousness or depression. Valerian has been usefully taken before an examination or a driving test!

PEPPERMINT

This is effective for treating digestive discomfort: it relieves indigestion, flatulence, constipation and nausea. Peppermint is also a good mind tonic, helping to clarify ideas and focus concentration. It is also helpful in alleviating the symptoms of colds and influenza. Peppermint and camomile tea is thought to be effective in reducing the pain of tension headaches and migraines.

VERVAIN

This is not only effective against depression but also strongly supports the detoxifying function of the liver. Its French name is still 'Herbe Sacre'; an old English name is 'Holy Wort' – it was one of the seven sacred herbs of the Druids. Today we know that the antispasmodic qualities of Verbena are largely due to the

Vervain

glycoside verbenalin. Recent Chinese research
has linked the plant with dilation of arteries in

the brain: a likely explanation of its usefulness in treating migraine, especially when this problem is accompanied by liver congestion. It is certainly of use to treat exhaustion and depression.

St John's wort

Also called *Hypericum perforatum*, St John's wort has analgesic and anti-inflammatory properties, with important local applications to neu-

St John's wort

ralgia and sciatica. Systemically, its sedative properties are based on the glycoside hypericin (a red pigment), which makes it applicable to neurosis and irritability. Many herbalists use it extensively as a background remedy.

LEMON BALM

This herb is both carminative and antispasmodic, and is active specifically on that part of the vagus nerve that may interfere with the harmonious functioning of the heart and the stomach. Recent research has indicated that the action of the volatile oil begins within the limbic system of the brain and subsequently operates directly upon the vagus nerve and all the organs that are innervated by it. Accordingly, neurasthenia (complete nervous prostration), migraine, and nervous gastropathy are amenable to its healing power.

LIME FLOWERS

These are thought to be helpful in controlling anxiety and hyperactivity. They are also effective for treating insomnia, high blood pressure and for soothing muscles and nerves.

BORAGE

This is an effective mind tonic, which helps to alleviate headaches, migraine and depression.

OATS

Oats is one of the great herbal restoratives of the nervous system. The plant contains a nervine alkaloid that is helpful in angina and in cardiac insufficiency. It has also been used in the treatment of addiction to morphine, narcotics, tobacco and alcohol.

Homeopathy

Put most simply, homeopathy is based on the belief that substances which are poisonous in large doses can be beneficial in small doses. Various substances can be taken in the form of pills, capsules, sachets of powder, sachets of granules or liquids. These homeopathic remedies can be bought in chemists and health shops, or obtained from a practitioner.

The principles of homeopathy where first expounded in 1796 by a German doctor, Christian Samuel Hahnemann. The fundamental principle, which he adopted (and which is still the mainstay of homeopathy), was 'Let like be cured by like'. He discovered that substances which are poisonous or toxic in their natural form can be used to cure, but will cure only that which they can cause. Guided by this 'law of healing', Hahnemann first prescribed substantial doses of a remedy, which often severely aggravated the symptoms, even when the eventual outcome was positive. To lessen the initial adverse reactions in his patients, Hahnemann diluted the dosage, using a method of his own devising, and found that this dilution did not diminish the medicinal power of the remedy but, in fact, enhanced it.

Many people come to a homeopath for help with a specific symptom or condition: arthritis, asthma, back pain, indeterminate aches and pains, menstrual problems, migraines, rheumatism, sciatica or skin conditions. The effect of a good homeopath, however, is to do more than simply help the symptom. Homeopathy is directed towards restoring the overall energy balance and treating the condition in an holistic way, so the patient will enjoy increased energy and vitality, better sleep and an improved appetite.

Homeopathic remedies are derived from a wide variety of sources, which include some pretty unusual substances, such as bee stings, snake venoms, arsenic, gold and silica, and even compounds from diseased tissue. Some 2000 different such remedies are in use. Even though these remedies are derived from often dangerous sources they are completely safe, having been diluted from the original substance (usually in alcohol or water) using Hahnemann's process, known as 'potentiation'. Various dilutions are used. A common one is known as 30C, and this indicates a dilution that would be represented by the figure 1 over 1 followed by 60 noughts (or $1 \times 10^{e-60}$) in scientific notation). It is the use of infinitesimal doses that is the most controversial aspect of homeopathy and the reason why many conventional doctors claim it functions only as a placebo. However, a number of controlled studies have been performed that show the effectiveness of homeopathic medicine in treating a number of diseases.

Taken in this diluted form, homeopathic remedies have no side effects whatsoever and are perfectly safe, nontoxic and non-addictive. They have all been tested extensively on humans (mostly practising homeopaths) to verify their safety and efficacy. Animal testing has never been used in homeopathy.

There is no conflict between conventional medicines and homeopathic remedies and, indeed, both systems of therapy may sometimes be used to complement each other. In most cases, when starting homeopathic treatment you should remain on your current conventional medicine. If you are taking conventional medicine (whether on prescription or not) you should tell your homeopath, who will discuss the situation with your doctor, if necessary, providing you give permission.

Homeopathy is a holistic therapy – that is, it investigates and treats the whole person rather than the specific problem presented by the patient. Because of this, your homeopath will enquire about many aspects of your condition – not just about the problems you present.

The initial consultation will take about an hour, and the homeopath will wish to hear all your symptoms and will enquire about many aspects of your health and lifestyle. These symptoms will then be analysed and the homeopath will decide upon a specific remedy to suit your particular needs. This analysis could take up to another hour, but you would not have to be present for this phase of the consultation. Once the homeopath has decided upon a remedy and potency (dilution) to be recommended, the material will be made up for you personally by the homeopath. The remedy may be provided immediately or it may take a day or two to prepare, in which case you can call back to pick it up or it will be posted to you.

Homeopathy is best when applied to conditions that are reversible – that is, anything that nature can cure or remove. Homeopathy cannot be used in place of surgery, but homeopathic remedies can be taken in conjunction with surgery and can be instrumental in making the surgery safer. They can also hasten postoperative healing.

In their basic form, homeopathic remedies are liquid formulations. They may be prescribed for you in this form, or they can be provided in tablet or granule form. In some cases, creams or lotions may be provided. Normally the form does not effect the action of the remedy, so if you prefer a particular form ask your homeopath. Remedies are taken on the tongue, if liquid, or held in the mouth to dissolve if in solid form. Creams and lotions are for external application. You should not eat or drink for 15 minutes before or after taking a homeopathic remedy, and you should avoid caffeinated coffee, camphor, menthol, peppermint and similar strong flavours while undergoing homeopathic treatment. Alcohol does not effect homeopathic remedies unless they are being taken for problems that are related to it.

Hypnotherapy

Because it can be used to treat conditions where psychological aspects are important, hypnotherapy is a valuable means of treating stress-related illnesses; although it is not clear how hypnosis works, and the links between hypnosis and entertainment have contributed to prejudice against its use as a therapeutic tool.

If you think of hypnosis as some sort of hocus pocus, however, think again. Increasing numbers of medical and mental health professionals now use hypnosis to overcome the pain of chronic headaches, backaches, childbirth, cancer, severe burns, dental phobias, and more. Some psychologists use hypnosis to help patients overcome bad habits, anxiety, phobias, and depression, even to help patients recall past events – although the accuracy of this recall is controversial. Family doctors have begun using hypnosis to treat psychosomatic illness, to control appetite, and to reduce the need for medication, or lower its dosage, in chronic illness.

The history of hypnosis dates back to the eighteenth century and the work of Franz Anton Mesmer, a physician from Germany. Hypnosis was used as pain relief, until anaesthetics became common. Although the word 'hypnosis' comes from the Greek word for sleep, hypnosis is actually an intense state of concentration, and this concentration is focused *inwardly*.

Although different therapists use different hypnosis techniques, the process today often begins with the patient closing his or her eyes and the therapist asking him or her to think relaxing thoughts. Often the person is asked to imagine a beautiful scene. As the therapist's soothing voice guides the patient down a path of deeper and deeper relaxation, the patient gradually becomes totally focused on the picture he or she sees in the mind – mirroring what happens when the patient is engrossed in a book or a daydream. All outside images and thoughts disappear.

In this state of focused concentration, the patient becomes suggestible. The therapist may then ask the patient to concentrate on his or her own breathing and other sensations inside the body. At this point, the therapist suggests ways that patients can accomplish individual goals.

Osteopathy

This is a technique that uses manipulation and massage to help distressed muscles and joints and make them work smoothly.

The profession began in 1892 when Andrew Taylor Still, an American farmer, inventor and doctor, opened the USA's first school of osteopathic medicine. He sought alternatives to the medical treatments of his day which he believed were ineffective as well as often harmful.

Still's new philosophy of medicine, based upon the teachings of Hippocrates, advocated that 'Finding health should be the purpose of a doctor. Anyone can find disease.' Like Hippocrates, Still recognised that the human

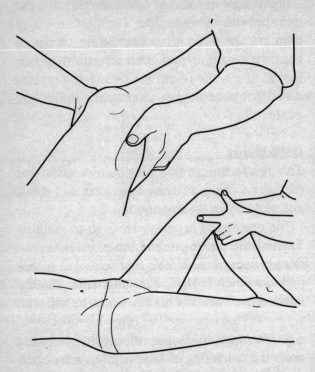

Diagnosis and treatment of the knee by osteopathy

body is a unit in which structure, function, mind and spirit all work together.

Still stressed the importance of preventing disease, eating properly and keeping fit. He studied the body's musculoskeletal system (the muscles, bones and joints) extensively and discovered how it works with other body systems to influence health. He taught that the body has the inherent ability to heal itself when all its systems function in harmony. To support his belief that body structure affects body function – and vice versa – he developed the unique 'hands-on' skill of osteopathic manipulative treatment to diagnose and treat structural problems. He emphasised the compassionate care and treatment of the person as a whole, not as a collection of symptoms or unrelated parts.

The philosophy and practices of A. T. Still, considered radical in the 1800s, are generally accepted principles of good medicine today.

Caring for a pet can help reduce stress levels

Pet therapy

The evidence is clear that owning and caring for a family pet can help to reduce stress levels. Pets provide their owners with unconditional love and loyalty. In return, the experience of caring for the animal imparts a sense of belonging and opportunities for play and amusement. Relationships with animals are largely free of the threats and responsibilities inherent in human intercourse. The rewards may not be so great,

Petting animals can reduce blood pressure

but for many animal lovers there can be no substitute for the emotional rewards of owning a
pet.

Physiological tests have shown that stroking
and petting animals can improve general health,
lower blood pressure, reduce anxiety and produce a reduction in stress levels.

Certain institutions, such as hospitals, old people's homes, and even prisons, have noticed an

improvement in their inmates' mental, physical and emotional health and behaviour when given access to animals.

Reflexology

Reflexology is a method for activating the natural healing resources of the body. Forms of reflexology have been in use for at least 3000 years (paintings depicting the art have been discovered in an Egyptian doctor's tomb dating back to 2330 BC). The science of reflexology as it is practised today was developed fairly recently, and its use as a complementary therapy has been on the increase ever since.

Around 1917, an American doctor called William Fitzgerald developed what he termed 'zone therapy', which treated the body as being divided into ten zones from head to foot, and asserted that by applying pressure to one area within a zone, one could dull pain in a corresponding area within the same zone.

In the 1930s, Eunice Ingham, an American physiotherapist, concluded in her zone therapy work that some areas of the body were more sensitive than others, the most sensitive of these being the feet. She proceeded to map the entire human body on the tops and bottoms of the feet, eventually discovering that by applying specific pressure with her thumbs and fingers she achieved therapeutic results far beyond simple pain reduction. Eunice Ingham dedicated the remainder of her life to developing and promoting reflexology into the successful healthcare alternative it is today.

Reflexology works on the principle that the body is divided into ten zones that run lengthwise from head to toe, where the reflex areas for all the organs, glands and body parts are found. Energy, sometimes referred to as Qi, kundalini, or the universal life force, also runs through these zones. Reflexologists believe that if this constant flow of energy is impeded by a blockage or congestion, illness sets in. A reflexologist, by using constant, rhythmic pressure on the reflexes of the patient's feet, breaks down the blockage, allowing the return of free-

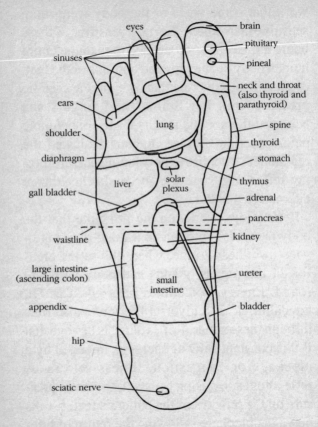

Major reflex points on the sole of the right foot

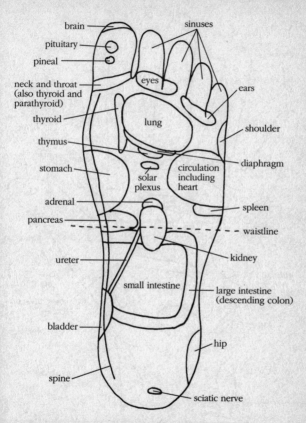

Major reflex points on the sole of the left foot

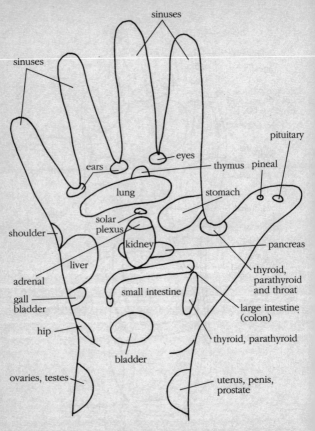

Major reflex points on the palm of the right hand

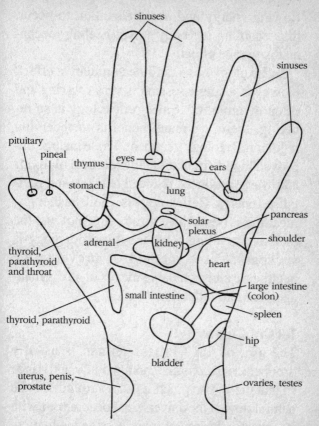

Major reflex points on the palm of the left hand

flowing energy and deep relaxation to occur, thus enabling the body's own healing mechanisms to take effect.

Reflexology has a definite cumulative effect. However, a single session is very relaxing and often invigorating. Since reflexology is so relaxing, there are many benefits to receiving regular reflexology treatment. These include improved blood circulation, the removal of toxins and waste products, reduced tension, and revitalised energy. Reflexology is a holistic therapy, meaning it treats the entire body – not just the part that is ailing. This is why reflexology is successful as a method of preventative healthcare and a valuable means of stress management and reduction.

Tai Chi Ch'uan

The aim of Tai Chi (the ch'uan is usually dropped) is to combine motion, unity and dance so that those who practise its art surrender to the natural flow of the universe and become one with it – exactly the aim of more passive meditation.

Tai Chi is a means of exploring the processes of mind and body through creative movement and reflects the I Ching belief that nature is always in motion. It is said to have originated with the meditation of a Taoist monk, Chang Sanfeng, who one day saw a magpie trying to attack a snake. The reptile teased the bird by writhing and curling in a spiral motion, always remaining just out of the bird's reach. Similar movements are now an integral part of Tai Chi.

In Tai Chi, the image of water symbolises the flow of energy, representing the flow of energy and the way it yields to the form of its container. Earth is seen as a link between person and planet. The use of circular forms of expression shows unity and containment.

It is not possible to learn Tai Chi from the pages of a book. Traditionally, the practice was handed down from master to pupil. Today most large towns offer Tai Chi classes, and anyone wishing to learn its ways and mysteries should join a group.

The classes always begin with a period of

太極拳

The Chinese characters for Tai Chi

meditative stillness, and then the pupils step forward on the right foot – an energy step with fire being visualised shooting from the palms of the hands. Then the energy is pulled back into the body and the weight transferred to the left foot, everyone now visualising water cascading over them. With the body turning to the left, the palms are rotated and curved back to the right. The body continues to turn to the right with both feet firmly fixed to the floor, then the left foot is brought round, returning the body to the centre.

Tai Chi is a process of self-discovery and, like yoga (*see* page 140), demonstrates the link between body movement and posture and contemplative states of being. In the words of one expert, Al Huang, who wrote the classic *Embrace Tiger, Return to Mountain*, 'Tai Chi is to help you get acquainted with your own sense of personal growth, the creative process of just being you.'

Useful Addresses

Stress Centres

First Assist
Britannia House
50 Great Charles Street
Queensway
Birmingham
B3 2LP
Tel: 0121 233 0202

Centre for Stress Management
156 Westcombe Hill
London
SE3 7DH
Tel: 0181 293 4114

Counselling Services

The British Association of
Counselling
1 Regent Place
Rugby
Warwickshire
CV21 2PJ
Tel: 01788 578 328

The British Association of
Psychotherapy
37 Mapesbury Road
London
NW2 4HJ
Tel: 0181 452 9823

Understanding Stress

MIND (National Association for Mental Health)
Grantha House
15–19 Broadway
Stratford
London
E15 UBQ
Tel: 0181 519 2122

Samaritans
10 The Grove
Slough
Berks.
SL1 1QP
Tel: 0345 909090
Admin: 01753 532 713

Complementary Medicine

Complementary Medicine
The Institute for Complementary Medicine
PO Box 194
London
SE16 1QZ
(Publishes a full register of complementary therapists)

The Natural Health
Network
Chardstock House
Chard Somerset
TA20 2TL
Tel: 01905 612 521

Council for Complementary and Alternative Medicine
Park House
206–208 Latimer Road
London
W10 6RE
Tel 0181 968 3862

Acupuncture

Association of Chinese Acupuncture/Traditional Chinese Medicine International (Registered UK/China) International School of Natural Medicine/BIFRAN (British and International Federation Register and Association of Naturopathy) Prospect House 2 Grove Lane Retford Nottinghamshire, DN22 6NA Tel/Fax: 01777 704 411 (Provides patients' clinics, education and registration in Chinese acupuncture, moxibustion and massage)

College of Traditional Acupuncture Tao House Queensway Royal Leamington Spa Warwickshire Tel: 01926 422 121

British Acupuncture Council Park House 206 Latimer Road London W10 6RE Tel: 0181 964 0222

Aromatherapy

International Federation of Aromatherapists Stanford House 2–4 Chiswick High Road London W4 1TH Tel: 0181 742 2605

Bach Flower Remedies

The Dr Edward Bach Foundation Mount Vernon Sotwell Wallingford Oxon. OX10 0PZ Tel: 01491 834 678

Understanding Stress

Colonic Hydrotherapy
Colonic International
Association
16 Drummond Ride
Tring
Hertfordshire
HP23 5DE

Homeopathy
The Homeopathic Trust
15 Clerkenwell Close
EC1R 0AA
(Send for a free copy of
leading magazine Health
and Homeopathy, and
info-pack on how to
obtain treatment on the
NHS and a list of
homeopathic doctors)

The Society of Homeopaths
2 Artizan Road
Northampton
NN1 4HU
Tel: 01604 621 400
Fax: 01604 622 622

The United Kingdom
Homeopathic Medical
Association
Administration Office
6 Livingstone Road
Gravesend, Kent
DA12 5DZ
Tel/Fax: 01474 560 336

Shiatsu
The European Shiatsu
School
Highbanks
Lockeridge
Marlborough
Wiltshire
SN8 4TQ
Tel: 01672 861 362

Yoga
The British Wheel of Yoga
1 Hamilton Place
Boston Road
Sleaford
Lincolnshire
NG34 7ES
Tel: 01529 303 233

Relationship Stress, Counselling and Support

Childline
Freepost 1111
London
N1 0BR
Freephone 0800 1111

CRUSE
Cruse House
126 Sheen Road
Richmond
Surrey
TW9 1UR
Tel: 0181 940 4818
(Bereavement counselling)

Gingerbread
16 Clerkenwell Close
London
EC12 0AN
Tel: 0171 336 8183
(Help for single parents)

National Association of
Widows
54–57 Allison Street
Digbeth
Birmingham
B5 5TH
Tel: 0121 643 8348

National Council for One
Parent Families
255 Kentish Town Road
London
NW5 2LX
Tel: 0171 267 1361

RELATE
Herbert Gray College
Little Church Street
Rugby
Warwicks
CV21 3AP
Tel: 01788 573 241

Health

Health Education Authority
Trevelyon House
Great Peter's Street
SW1P 2HW
Tel: 0171 222 5300

Alcoholism

Alcohol Concern
Waterbridge House
32–36 Lemon Street
SE1 0EE
Tel: 0171 928 7377

Alcoholics Anonymous
PO Box 1
Stonebow House
Stonebow
York
YO1 7NJ

Drug Addiction

CITA (Council for Involuntary Tranquilliser Addiction)
Cavendish House
Brighton Road
Waterloo
Liverpool
L22 5NG
Tel: 0151 949 0102

The Doddington and Rollo
Community Association
Unit 37
Charlotte Despard Avenue
Battersea
SE11 5JE
Tel: 0171 498 4680

TASHA (Tranquilliser and Anxiety Self-Help Association)
Tel: 0181 569 9933

Smoking

ASH (Action on Smoking
and Health)
109 Gloucester Place
London
W1N 7RH
Tel: 0171 935 3519

Stress-related Illnesses

Arthritis

The Arthritic Association
First Floor Suite
2 Hyde Gardens
Eastbourne
BN21 4PN
(Provides dietary guidance
with homeopathic and
herbal treatment to help
relieve those suffering
from arthritis and rheumatism)

Asthma

National Asthma Cam-
paign
Providence House
Providence Place
London
N1 0NT
Tel: 0171 226 2260

Diabetes

British Diabetic Associa-
tion
10 Queen Anne Street
London
W1M 0BD
Tel: 0171 323 1531

National Diabetes Founda-
tion
177a Tennison Road
London
SE25 5NF
Tel: 0181 656 5467

Understanding Stress

Heart Disease

British Heart Foundation
14 Fitzharding Street
London
W1H 4DH
Tel: 0171 935 0185

The Coronary Prevention
Group
42 Store Street
London
WC1E 7DB
Tel: 0171 580 1070

Migraine

Migraine Action Association
178a High Road
Byfleet, West Byfleet
Surrey, KT14 7ED
Tel: 01932 352 468

Migraine Trust
45 Great Ormond Street
London
WC1N 3HZ
Tel: 0171 831 4818

PMS

National Association for
Premenstrual Syndrome
7 Swift's Court
High Street
Seal
Kent
TN15 0EG
Tel: 01732 760 011

Skin Disorders

National Eczema Society
163 Eversholt Place
London
NW1 1BU
Tel: 0171 388 4097

The Psoriasis Association
7 Milton Street
Northampton
NN2 7JG
Tel: 01604 711 129